Your Cricketing Score Card

Dedication

Introduction

Part One: ICC World Cup, India 2023

Kiwis hand England a painful World Cup lesson

Malan century sees England off and running at the World Cup

England shocked and humbled by Afghanistan

Champions England on brink of losing World Cup Crown

Early exit looms for an embarrassing England at the World Cup

World Cup can't end quickly enough for a sorry England

Australia hammer final nail into England's World Cup coffin

Maxwell breaks Afghan hearts with an innings for the ages

The Afghan dream is over

Kohli and Shami guide India to one win from destiny

Captain Cummins leads Australia into World Cup Final

Australia spoil the Indian coronation to become World Champions

Part Two: Winter tour to India, 2024

India in the box seat after day 1 in Hyderabad

India forge ahead on "Republic Day"

The audacity of Pope gives England hope

Ben Stokes and the Patron Saint of Lost Causes

Jaiswal century edges India ahead on day 1 in Visakhapatnam

"Boom Boom Bumrah!"

Shubman Gill bats England into an impossible mission

History prevails as India level the series

Milestones galore as India take charge on day 1 in Rajkot

Duckett century signals spectacular England fightback in Rajkot

Revolutionaries Routed in Rajkot

India rampage to thunderous victory in Rajkot

Root grinds a priceless century for England on day 1 in Ranchi

Bashir tightens the screw as England dominate in Ranchi

England in a spin. India now favourites in Ranchi Test

India too strong for plucky England in Ranchi

Kuldeep Yadav spins England out of control in Dharamshala

India are over the Himalayan Mountains and far, far away

Anderson the record breaker but Ashwin spins England to defeat

Aussies "possums in the headlights" as Kiwis chase for victory

World Champion Aussies break Kiwi hearts again

Sundries on the Scorecard

Dedication

For my Mother and Father,
Maureen and Patrick

Introduction

Thank you for taking a chance on my third and cricketing hat-trick of books on the grandest game in all the world. I hope you enjoy the ride.

Stephen Blackford, 18th March 2024

"To me, cricket is a simple game. Keep it simple, and just go out and play"

Shane Warne

"Cricket is basically baseball on valium"

Robin Williams

Part One: ICC World Cup, India 2023

The "Team of Destiny" fall one short to a gang of mates and World Test Champions

Kiwis hand England a painful World Cup lesson

New Zealand v England, 5th October 2023

ENGLAND 282–9
NEW ZEALAND 283–1 *(win by 9 wickets)*

Oh dear.

Well this wasn't quite what England captain Jos Buttler envisioned for his team's opening day defence of the World Cup crown they won *"by the barest of margins"* against today's opponents New Zealand four short years ago!

Being defeated by 9 wickets with still the thick end of 14 overs remaining and both opposition batsmen at the crease unbeaten with a century each to their name in a 273 run partnership, is as comprehensive and demoralising as it sounds, but here's hoping the after match words of both an ex England captain and the current incumbent prove wise before the event, and ahead of the long seven week cricketing road that lies before us, and a return to the incredible Narendra Modi Stadium in Ahmedabad for the World Cup Final on 19th November.

Joe Root, easily England's most impressive performer today with 77 runs from 86 balls received, and the anchor of mid innings partnerships with Harry Brook and Jos Buttler that threatened to set the England batting innings alight but which flickered and ultimately died early cricketing deaths, called for *"calm"* post match whilst captain Buttler pragmatically said today was *"just one loss at the start of a long tournament"*. Both players too echoed a constant sentiment of there being *"bumps"* in this particular cricketing road and although this is only the first game of a very long World Cup, today wasn't so much of a bump but a badly bloodied nose in a fight for the defence of their World Champion crown.

From the fall of their first wicket at 40–1 and Dawid Malan presenting Kiwi Matt Henry with the first of 3 deserved wickets at the cost of 48 runs, England would continually establish double digit batting partnerships throughout their middle order (24, 30, 24, 70 and 33) but as these figures would suggest, batsmen *"got in"* and established before, in the quixotic language of this grandest of all games, they got themselves out too.

In and out.

Out, and back in again.

Jonny Bairstow's first scoring shot was a mighty boundary 6, and in the first over of the contest too, before he followed Malan back into the Pavilion to give Mitchell Santner the first of his 2 wickets for the cost of just 37 runs. Harry Brook, rightly in the team on merit and for his attacking verve and seemingly nerveless disposition, crashed the bowling of eventual *"Man of the Match"* candidate Rachin Ravindra to all parts of this vast cricketing oval in Ahmedabad before falling or *"giving his wicket away"* like so many of his colleagues today by *"checking"* or not fully committing to the shot and looping simple high catches to eager Kiwi's patrolling the boundary. Buttler and Bairstow were equally culpable in this regard too with Root dying by the reverse sweep sword he lives by and when Moeen Ali fell for just 11 to a piece of bowling *"magic"* (according to West Indian commentator Ian Bishop) part-time off spin bowler Glenn Phillips was on his way to a brilliant 2 wickets for just 17 runs conceded, England were tottering on 118-4 and their eventual total of 282 was creditable, but at least 70 runs shy of being competitive. To the victors, the spoils, and a thoroughly deserved and comprehensive win for New Zealand it was too. When you consider that bowling spearhead Matt Henry (and main strike bowler due to the injury absence of Tim Southee) scalped 3 wickets and regular and/or part-time spin bowling accounted for another 5 England wickets along the way, it was a near perfect 50 overs in the field from the Kiwis.

Then, even if their legendary batsman Kane Williamson was fit and playing rather than watching from the stands, he wouldn't have even been required to wield his batting willow in anger as the always impressive Devon Conway scooted his way to 100 from just 83 balls received and current wunderkind Rachin Ravindra, nearly 10 years his junior at just 23 years of age, needed 1 less delivery for his personal century on his way to a stunning 123 not out from just 96 balls received. Conway perhaps edges the *"Man of the Match"* stakes by *"carrying his bat"* throughout the innings for a mightily impressive 152 not out from just 121 balls received but regardless, this was as comprehensive a team win as can possibly be imagined. Chris Woakes and Mark Wood, this Summer's Ashes heroes in their vain attempt to wrest the urn from New Zealand's noisy neighbours Australia, were, in the cricketing vernacular, *"carted"* to all parts of the Narendra Modi Stadium and only bowled a combined 11 overs between them for a staggering century of runs conceded. No England bowler had an economy rate less than 6 and hence, conceded at least a run every ball bowled and yes it is *"just one loss at the start of a long tournament"*, but Ben Stokes' Lazarus like powers of recovery are needed and needed fast as although two of the minnows of the tournament lie in wait for their next two games (Bangladesh and Afghanistan), they still have to play my arguable favourites for the tournament India, as well as bitter neighbours Pakistan, let alone South Africa or an Australian team in the middle of yet another rebuild.

I have England second favourites for the tournament behind India and ahead of Pakistan in a top 3, but New Zealand have shown once again why they've played in both consecutive World Cup Finals since 2015 and why they might well achieve a hat-trick of sorts come mid November.

Time will tell.

It always does.

Malan century sees England off and running at the World Cup

Bangladesh v England, 10th October 2023

ENGLAND *364-9*
BANGLADESH *227 all out*

England win by 137 runs

After only 90 minutes sleep between watching my Los Angeles Dodgers lose once more to the Arizona Diamondbacks on the rocky road to a World Series they are clearly destined not to reach and the beginning of England's highly expected thumping of Bangladesh, the walls were beginning to bend, I'd clearly drunk too much late night and early morning tea, and England's Reece Topley was on the rampage with early wickets and narrowly missing out on a World Cup hat-trick on his way to 4 Bangladesh wickets for the cost of just 43 runs.

With the heavy cricketing underdogs already 26–3 chasing England's unreachable target of 365 runs to win, I collected my son for an amble in some unexpected warm October sunshine on the banks of the River Severn in the historic toy-town of Ironbridge, and after feeding some hungry swans and ducks we treated ourselves to some sweets from the town's *"Old Fashioned Sweet Shop"* before some piping hot fish and chips beside the *"Grand Old Lady"* and the world's oldest iron bridge.

England were destined to win easily, so why worry?

Since we were last together, the Los Angeles Dodgers have thrown their almost unbeatable seasonal record out of the play-offs window yet again and with England experiencing a 72 hour spell of unseasonably warm October weather, I treated myself to another morning and early afternoon in Ironbridge but rather than my beautiful son for company I came armed with a tripod and a video camera as I took up residence on a rickety old fishing peg on the banks of the River Severn to record four videos for my Youtube channel that one day, one fine day, will melt the internet and probably the very fabric of the space/time continuum too. The *"Grand Old Lady"* sure provides the most perfect of backdrops and with a still river barely moving, the most incredible of reflections too.

Yesterday I was larking around in front of a video camera, trying to make myself smile as well as hawking around a self-published book on football that I couldn't be more proud of if you paid me. Today was the feeding of swans and ducks with a kid in a *Dr Who* t-shirt.

Bliss.

Since we were last together the world has taken another sharp right turn into the macabre with the horrifying sights emerging from Palestine and Israel. As ever we're expected and demanded to pick a side from our Overlords who control both teams in this unspeakable murderous mayhem of which only they benefit. Fear. The spectacle of fear. The *"theatre"* of war. The one sided propaganda for the one sided war against all of us. The much missed American comedian Bill Hicks had it right when he questioned whether we, the indoctrinated, propagandised, disaster capitalism loving *"West"* were in fact the *"Evil Empire"* and we are, and we're seemingly on the brink of World War III for the 78th year in succession.

So with the walls bending and taking shape all around me I went for a stroll along the banks of the River Severn. Ironbridge, much like the grand old game of cricket, does wonders for the soul.

Talking of cricket, since we were last together another plucky underdog in the shape of the Netherlands have been beaten, but not trounced and embarrassed, by both Pakistan and New Zealand, with the Kiwis holding a 100% record after two games and their demolition act inflicted upon England five days ago. Bangladesh defeated Afghanistan in the battle of the minnows before on the same October Saturday, South Africa and Sri Lanka combined for an astonishing, record breaking 754 total runs, with Rassie van der Dussen and Quinton de Kock South African centurions both, alongside World Cup record breaker Aiden Markram with his faintly ridiculous 106 from just 54 balls received.

Australia, already written off by your favourite cricket correspondent and clearly a man who doesn't learn by his past cricketing mistakes, reduced tournament favourites India to 2–3 in their chase of just 200 runs for victory before crowd darling Virat Kohli and KL Rahul dug their team out of a huge hole to an impressive, and seemingly imposing 6 wicket victory, but this game was far from the one-sided Indian triumph inked in the forever scorecards of this World Cup.

So to today, and following a steady opening century partnership between *"Man of the Match"* Dawid Malan and Jonny Bairstow, England romped their way to an opening World Cup win without any major scares.

Yorkshiremen Jonny Bairstow and Joe Root are *"in the runs"* to use a cricketing phrase of yore, with Root racking up an impressive 159 total runs across the 2 games so far and of course Dawid Malan proving his worth once more at the top of the batting order with 140 from just 107 balls received today, and the *"anchor"* of an innings that rather fell away following his dismissal as England collapsed to a symmetrical 66–6 in the final 10 overs of their innings to close on 364–9 and some distance from the expected 400+ with Malan at the crease unbeaten, and the score standing at 266–1. England scored just 98 runs for the fall of their last 8 wickets in 13 overs, but it mattered not. Shoriful Islam impressed me once again with the ball for Bangladesh, as he did during their winter tour to New Zealand of 2021/2022. He ripped the heart out of the England middle order batting, scalping the wickets of Joe Root, Jos Buttler and Liam Livingstone on his way to an unsuccessful attempt at a World Cup hat-trick and Liton Das anchored his team's run chase with an impressive 76 runs from 66 balls received. Wicket-keeper Mushfiqur Rahim and Towhid Hridoy combined mid-innings with 90 total runs between them, however 365 runs to win was always an impossible dream, but Bangladesh will win again in this tournament in the coming weeks. For England, it's Afghanistan on Sunday before a humdinger of a game in prospect with South Africa the following Saturday.

This cricket World Cup is officially off and running.

England shocked and humbled by Afghanistan

England v Afghanistan, 15th October 2023

AFGHANISTAN 284 all out
ENGLAND 215 all out

Afghanistan (shock the world) and win by 69 runs

Well this wasn't in the script for the defending World Champions but whomever penned this particular sporting screenplay cannot be accused of writing an unrealistic story for this was a thoroughly deserved and comprehensive victory straight from the very top of World Cup shocks of all time. Perhaps, as I'm in a sportingly romantic mood, we should turn to Afghanistan spin bowler Mujeeb Ur Rahman as the first of our cricketing storytellers as first he clubbed 28 quick runs from just 16 balls received at the end of his team's mightily impressive stint with the bat, before bowling an over from the cricketing Gods at England's Chris Woakes that was pure theatre, skill, guile, endeavour, mystery and entertainment writ large, before he dismantled Woakes' *"castle"* of stumps behind him.

My goodness, this was cricket in its grandest form, and Mujeeb would add England's only guiding light yesterday in Harry Brook to his tally of wickets that also included Joe Root, and with Woakes and Brook dismissed in such quick fashion, England were 169–8 and staring down the barrel of arguably the greatest shock in cricket World Cup history.

Although run out unnecessarily by his captain when cruising along and 80 not out, 21 year old Rahmanullah Gurbaz has quite the story to tell too as he, in the cricketing vernacular, *"only dealt in boundaries"* as he clubbed and carted around a woeful and out of form Chris Woakes (and any and every England bowler who deigned to bowl at him!) on his way to a 33 ball half century and 80 from just 57 balls before his unfortunate demise. Where Afghanistan wobbled and threatened to collapse mid-innings, up stepped wicket-keeper batsman Ikram Alikhil who calmly steadied the innings by rotating the strike and keeping the scoreboard ticking along with a 61 ball half century and ultimately a well played and innings saving 58 from 66 balls received. A couple of hours later, the 23 year old wicket-keeper from Kabul would snag a sharp catch behind the stumps to extinguish England's last hope in Harry Brook, and we haven't accounted yet for the part played in our cricketing story for the ages of Mohammad Nabi (2 wickets for 16 runs) or crowd darling Rashid Khan (3 wickets for 37 runs).

Nabi grabbed the vital early wicket of Dawid Malan that consigned England to a faltering 68–3 before Khan, so impressive in his early spell of bowling, returned to rip out 3 late order England wickets, with the dismissal to remove Liam Livingstone an absolute gem.

Coached by ex England international Jonathan Trott, he was remarkably level headed during the after match interviews and even suggested, without his tongue in cheek, that this wasn't a *"perfect performance"* and he demanded his players build on this, only their second all time victory in a World Cup, but you could just hear the pride seeping from his every pore. His players though were rather more emotional, with both Rashid Khan and Mujeeb Ur Rahman dedicating this win to the families back home in Afghanistan still dealing with the unimaginable fallout from the recent earthquake, with Rashid Khan emotionally stating *"cricket is something that brings joy to the people back home"* before recognising the achievement in defeating the World Champions and hoping *"this win will put a little bit of smile on their faces"* as so many thousands of his compatriots endeavour to rebuild their homes, their lives and their very existence.

So what of the defending Champions and a thoroughly dismantled and badly beaten England? England captain Jos Buttler was magnanimous in conceding *"Afghanistan outplayed us today"* and perhaps more tellingly *"this is a tough loss to take"*.

It sure is.

It's also the bitter truth to our sporting tale and a loss that leaves England precariously hanging on to a fading hope of qualification for the Semi-Finals after their second defeat in three games. I already have three Semi-Final berths sewn up in the shape of the hosts India, New Zealand and South Africa, with England now battling with Pakistan, Australia and, to a lesser extent, Sri Lanka, for that fourth and final spot. At the time of writing, Australia and Sri Lanka are facing off in Lucknow and whilst not strictly an elimination game, today's loser will almost certainly be out with zero points and three consecutive losses to their name, and England, only two points better off at this stage of the competition, still have to play both of today's opponents as well as Pakistan and an unbeatable looking India. The signs do not look promising for Jos Buttler and his England team and up next, they have the mighty, free scoring South Africa to deal with.

Saturday's game is HUGE.

Since were we last together, my Los Angeles Dodgers did indeed throw their incredible seasonal record out of the play-offs window together with their tickets to baseball's October *"Big Dance"* and the break for international football continues to be the second biggest suck in sport and just below the Orwellian VAR system that our Overlords are determined to facilitate the final death throes of Pele's *"Beautiful Game"*.

Returning to India and a cricket World Cup they are seemingly destined to win, on the same day that England firmly dispensed with the spirited fight of Bangladesh, Pakistan chased an incredible 345 runs to defeat Sri Lanka by 6 wickets, South Africa smashed Australia by a thumping 134 runs, New Zealand brushed aside Bangladesh by 8 wickets to retain their 100% winning start to the tournament and the hosts India chased 273 to defeat Afghanistan by 8 wickets with 15 overs still remaining before they inflicted a horrible chastening to Pakistan by chasing 192 to win, achieving this comfortably by 7 wickets, and with fully 20 overs to spare! Although a one-sided affair, this was my game of the tournament so far. A wholly partisan Indian crowd of over 100,000 packed into the Narendra Modi Stadium in Ahmedabad and with Pakistan 155–2 and their hero Babar Azam exactly 50 not out, the noisy din of a celebratory crowd had been replaced by a low and quietened murmur.

An hour of exhilarating cricket later, Pakistan had spectacularly collapsed to 191 all out, losing their final 8 wickets for just 36 total runs in the process, and the ear-splitting din returned as they roared on an imperious innings from their captain Rohit Sharma and the very man who is firm favourite to be lifting the World Cup trophy in this very stadium, and in just over a month's time.

Since we were last together the world continues to turn at an ugly angle with fairy tales of countries having the right to defend themselves as they obliterate their neighbours from our earthly map. One war replaces another in the forever war of our consciousness. Ghoulish, wraith like creatures appear constantly on our Telescreens to defend the barbarity of war, the deletion of human rights and a blind eye is cast to the inhuman destruction of untold hundreds of thousands of human lives as we're told to pick a side, wave a flag and not trust our own lying eyes.

We never learn. Perhaps there's a strong argument to be made that we're simply not permitted to.

And this rambling fool can only despair at our collective plight.

Champions England on brink of losing World Cup Crown

South Africa v England, 21st October 2023

SOUTH AFRICA 399–7
ENGLAND 170 all out

South Africa win by 229 runs

Well this wasn't supposed to happen was it!

On a sporting Saturday towards the end of October, the mighty nations of England and South Africa faced off not once but twice, but whereas the England rugby team would lose a World Cup Semi-Final in Paris they'd largely dominate and be incredibly, incredibly unlucky to lose by one single point in the dying embers of a physically brutal encounter, they were rather embarrassed by a rampant South Africa who looked light years ahead of a tired, injury plagued and completely out of sorts England who now stare into the abyss of an early elimination from a World Cup they are the proud holders of, and currently 9th in a cricketing table of 10 behind tournament lightweights the Netherlands, Sri Lanka and Bangladesh.

For 45 minutes this morning England were outstanding. Opening bowlers Reece Topley and David Willey used the new ball expertly with Topley snagging the early prized wicket of Quinton de Kock with only the second delivery of the contest and Reeza Hendricks and Rassie van der Dussen had no alternative but to, in the cricketing vernacular, *"dig in"*, preserve their wickets and ride out the early storm. Another minor injury to Topley saw him leave the field early (he returned later in the innings with 2 wickets but at a heavy cost of runs against him) and with his early departure, the storm passed, and Hendricks and van der Dussen made hay.

Hendricks, only in the team 45 minutes before the start of play due to the illness of captain Temba Bavuma, crashed 9 boundary 4's and 3 boundary clearing 6's on his way to an impressive 85 from just 75 balls received as he shared a 121 run partnership with van der Dussen for the 2nd wicket, the senior man rattling a run-a-ball 60 before both South African batsmen fell to the leg spin bowling of Adil Rashid, England's best bowler again on a day you had zero reason whatsoever to attach the label *"best"* to anything connected with England Cricket.

In an innings typified by dominating batting partnerships, stand-in skipper Aiden Markram knocked a run-a-ball 42 in league with Heinrich Klaasen, before the big hitting Klaasen was joined by the gangly fast bowler Marco Jansen, and their 151 run partnership was something to behold, as well as a chastening and embarrassing couple of hours for a tired looking England completely and utterly out on their feet. Jansen finished the innings on a remarkable 75 not out from just 42 balls received but even this display paled into the shadows of a quite extraordinary cricketing *"knock"* from Klaasen.

The 32 year old from Pretoria reached his half century from 40 balls received and his century from 61. Read that again! If my mathematics are correct, he went from 50 to 100 in just 21 balls! Furthermore, and perhaps the most sobering and overwhelming statistic of them all this morning, was South Africa smashing 131 runs from the final 9 overs of their innings, and at a rate of over 2 runs per ball received.

Staggering stuff.

Setting England 400 to win was fantasy land stuff even before England crumpled, crumbled and collapsed to defeat, and in just 22 overs.

England disappeared out of sight as they collapsed from 18–0 to 100–8 in just 14 overs bowled and had it not been for a 70 run partnership for the final wicket between Gus Atkinson (35 from 21 balls) and Mark Wood (43 from 17 balls), they could have lost by an even bigger and more embarrassing margin than the already, and final, difference between the two teams of a gargantuan 229 runs. Again on a day when *"best"* could not be applied anywhere near the England cricket team, this is a little unfair on Atkinson and especially the lusty and entertaining blows from Mark Wood who simply took aim and crashed 5 almighty boundary clearing 6's and 2 boundary 4's in his 17 ball cameo at the end of an innings all of his teammates will wish to forget in a hurry and quite frankly, they have to.

Still a mathematical possibility of qualification, and still a light shines of possibility should they clamber their way into a Semi-Final spot, but this England team looks fragile, *"cooked"* in the cricketing vernacular, and abject in any language you wish. Sri Lanka are up next on Thursday in a *"must win game"*, a moniker that applies to EVERY game from hereon in, including the tussles with old foes Australia, India and Pakistan.

England are out but in the quirky nature and indeed language of cricket, they're still in. They'll be out soon enough, and then the inquest shall commence.

Elsewhere in the World Cup, New Zealand trounced Afghanistan by 139 runs and India defeated Bangladesh by 7 wickets, thus setting up today's cricketing battle of the final two undefeated teams in the tournament.

At the time of writing, India need a further 128 runs from 24 overs (crowd darling Virat Kohli 26 not out) and New Zealand a further 7 Indian wickets in which to preserve their respective 100% records. Australia have finally got their tournament underway after brushing aside a weak looking Sri Lanka by 5 wickets as well as smashing 367 total runs against a Pakistan team they eventually defeated by 62 runs.

Pakistan remain an enigmatic presence at this World Cup, flattering to deceive or mightily impressive, and they would rue a dropped catch or three on their way to eventual defeat by Australia and especially spilling a cricketing *"dolly"* of a catch that would have dismissed David Warner on just 10 before the Paddington born fighting alley cat would smash his way to an incredible 163 from just 124 balls received.

You wait around for a seismic shock at the World Cup and just 2 days after England's humiliation at the hands of Afghanistan came the Netherlands thoroughly deserved and dominating victory against England's victors today South Africa, and despite a number of these results going in favour of England clambering the table towards the top 4 positions, today's result happened, and on the back of each nation receiving an ignominious defeat on the cricketing field of play, I can only see South Africa squeezing into the Semi-Finals, and England trudging off home early.

Early exit looms for an embarrassing England at the World Cup

Sri Lanka v England, 26th October 2023

ENGLAND 156 all out
SRI LANKA 160–2

Sri Lanka win by 8 wickets

It was 9.30am local UK time and with the beginnings of a long Winter ahead, the perfect opportunity to start the sporting day nestled beneath a warming duvet and a piping hot cup of tea for company. The first ball of the day from Dilshan Madushanka was dispatched back past him by England opening batsman Jonny Bairstow on a fast looking and runs filled wicket in Bengaluru, racing across an equally fast looking outfield for 3 runs. So far, so cricketing unremarkable. But even a world away and snuggled beneath a pleasingly warm duvet it was easy to see that the delivery had brushed Bairstow's pad before his bat followed suit with a more firm and decisive contact.

Sri Lankan captain Kusal Mendis couldn't be persuaded to refer this to the TV Umpire but had he done so, rather than England being 3–0 from the game's very first delivery, they would have in fact been 0–1, and Jonny Bairstow trudging back from whence he came to the Pavilion, and with a cricketing *"duck"* for company.

For 30 minutes Bairstow and fellow opening batsman Dawid Malan made hay, punishing any wide and wayward bowling for repeated boundary 4's and at 45–0, England had made a rock solid start in the first of a series of *"must win"* games that any defeat will see them ignominiously dumped from the World Cup as limp and lame defending Champions.

An hour later they were 88–5 from just 19 overs, openers Malan and Bairstow followed back to the Pavilion by single scores from captain Jos Buttler, Liam Livingstone and Joe Root, with the ex-captain ridiculously run out in a calamitous hour for the defending Champions.

So I went to the cinema instead!

"Five Nights at Freddy's" was the choice of my beautiful son who'd eagerly booked the tickets many weeks ago, and whilst this horror and platform genre swap from the gaming world to the cinema screen was a worthy addition to the canon of films from the Blumhouse production line, I was rather hoping I'd return to an England fighting for their cricketing lives and defending a total of perhaps 220 after Mark Wood had yet again bailed out his batsmen with a lusty half century full of boundary clearing 6's.

Alas I returned to the grave news that England had already been defeated, some 45 minutes before I even returned from the cinema, and only Test captain Ben Stokes provided any resistance whatsoever with 43 as England limped to an embarrassing 156 all out.

David Willey snagged 2 early Sri Lankan wickets and at 23–2 it was arguably a contest, but 77 not out from Pathum Nissanka and a less than a run-a-ball 65 from Sadeera Samarawickrama consigned England to their fourth defeat in five games, and with 25 overs still to be bowled.

25 overs!

Five Nights at Freddy's?

How about five games, four defeats, three heavy and embarrassing ones too, and only the rank outsiders Netherlands preventing England from tenth place out of ten in a World Cup table that makes for incredibly embarrassing reading for all concerned. The horror show will almost certainly continue on Sunday with a heavy defeat from the seemingly unbeatable India, and this will mathematically end any hopes of a recovery even Lazarus would proclaim to be absurd.

Since we were last together, and avoiding comment on the wider world this time as I'm as sick and frustrated at the tired old screenplay being played out on our collective telescreens as you are, Sri Lanka gained their first win of the tournament with a 5 wicket win over the Netherlands and today's 8 wicket demolition of England sees them climb the table into 5th place behind a resurgent Australia who thumped the same Netherlands team by an astonishing 309 runs. This game was a joy to watch as my favourite Australian fighting alley cat David Warner used a couple of his feline lives on his way to a blistering half century from just 40 balls received before leaping for joy on the achieving of his century from just 91 balls received.

Then it became the Glenn Maxwell show!

The beneficiary of an extra cricketing *"life"* when on 26, the 35 year old from Kew played the most outrageous of reverse sweeps and scoops on his way to 50 from just 27 balls before smashing the next 13 balls to all parts of Delhi on his way to a record breaking and otherworldly century from just 40 balls received. It was an innings for the ages and an innings of pure sporting wonder.

India were pushed all the way in the battle of the unbeaten teams by New Zealand before triumphing by 4 wickets, Bangladesh made South Africa work above and beyond the call of cricketing duty for their 149 run triumph, but leaving the best for the very last, step forward Afghanistan.

Set 283 to win by a Pakistan team who were their usual contradiction of spectacular then incredibly ragged, the record books will show an 8 wicket victory for the minnows and heavy underdog Afghanistan, but the longer story is even more impressive than that. Whilst Ibrahim Zadran played somewhat of an *"anchor"* role with 87 runs from 113 balls received, his opening batting partner Rahmanullah Gurbaz once again demonstrated the excitement circling around this 21 year old with a brilliant half century from just 35 balls and eventual 65 from 53 total balls received. At their combined demise and the score 190–2, Afghanistan needed 93 runs from 99 balls remaining.

Step forward Rahmat Shah (77 not out) and captain Hashmatullah Shahidi who not only bludgeoned 48 not out from 45 balls received, but also led his side and nation to a famous, thoroughly deserved, and comprehensive win for the ages and another huge shock at this World Cup.

An 8 wicket victory sounds and looks impressive enough, but this was far, far more than that.

Neither Afghanistan nor Bangladesh will qualify for the top 4 Semi-Final spots but I'm cheering them on from afar, and England will soon be home to experience the beginnings of a cold Winter ahead amid recriminations and rancour, and the beginning of a fresh new page in England one-day cricket going forward.

See you on Sunday.

World Cup can't end quickly enough for a sorry England

India v England, 29th October 2023

INDIA 229-9
ENGLAND 129 all out

India win by 100 runs

Post-match, England skipper Jos Buttler was rightly proud of his bowlers David Willey, Adil Rashid and Chris Woakes the pick of the bunch with 7 wickets between them, and that they *"fancied themselves"* after restricting India to a lowly 229-9 from their 50 overs amid a cacophonous din of air horns inside the Lucknow stadium.

At 30-0 and needing exactly 200 further runs for an improbable and unlikely victory against the hosts and overwhelming favourites for the World Cup, one would imagine the England captain cast more than a hopeful glance towards a victory that would keep his team's remotely slim chances of a Semi-Final spot alive.

25 excruciating overs later, England were 98–8 and their collapse of 8 wickets for the addition of just 68 total runs was as the skipper said *"the same old story"* and England are bottom of the table, out of the tournament they were the defending Champions of, and face the prospect of *"dead rubber"* games against old foes Australia and Pakistan, and one begins to worry they'll be pushed all the way by tournament minnows the Netherlands too.

All in all, this World Cup can't end quickly enough for this sorry, abject England team.

Inserted into bat, India were reliant upon a 91 run partnership between skipper Rohit Sharma and wicket-keeper KL Rahul and with their demise came the surreal sound of silence as the air horns were temporarily quietened. A run-a-ball 49 from Suryakumar Yadav ensured both the air horns returned as well as his team eventually reaching a below par total of just 229, easily 75 runs short of a truly competitive total and England firmly in the game. Rohit Sharma's classy 87 runs from 101 balls received was easily the game's one true highlight and what a joy it is to see the 36 year old from Nagpur wield his cricketing willow. 10 boundary 4's and 3 boundary clearing 6's, it was an innings deserving of a century and I for one cannot wait to see him don the whites of Test Match cricket for England's early 2024 tour of his home country.

Rohit Sharma's batting elegance is a thing of cricketing beauty and albeit painfully, so was the way his pace and spin bowlers dismantled a sorry looking England.

Mohammed Shami (4–22) and Jasprit Bumrah (3–32) *"top and tailed"* the England batting order with ferocious spells of fast bowling that saw Shami making a mess of Jonny Bairstow and Ben Stokes cricketing *"castle"* behind them as Bumrah did likewise to Malan's stumps before trapping Joe Root *"plumb"* LBW for a golden duck, and an immediate and disconsolate trudge back to the Pavilion from whence he came. From 30–0 England had lost their top 4 premier batsmen for the addition of just 9 runs and whilst *"the man with the golden arm"* according to local Indian TV commentators Mohammed Shami snagged the wicket of Moeen Ali for 15, his spinning bowling mates of Kuldeep Yadav and Ravindra Jadeja brilliantly ripped out the remaining heart of the England batting order. Yadav's delivery that bowled Jos Buttler was a true gem, the England captain playing an ungainly nothing of a shot before his stumps were splayed everywhere and his delivery to remove Liam Livingstone (England's top scorer with 27) was a thing of cricketing beauty too. Shami came back to make a mess of Adil Rashid's stumps, Bumrah did likewise with his first ball to Mark Wood, and England are out of the World Cup with 3 games still to play.

Cue the air horns!

Since we were last together, my lifelong football team of choice Liverpool are back to winning ways and back on an undefeated run, South Africa are rugby World Champions after remarkably winning their Quarter-Final, Semi-Final and Final by one, single solitary point in each game, and a pulsating and quite brilliant Final on Saturday in Paris against New Zealand, and baseball's *"Big Dance"* of the World Series is underway with the score standing at 1–1 after 2 matches in this best of 7 season ending spectacular. Here we have the *"Rangers"* of Texas as favourites over the *"Diamondbacks"* of Arizona with the underdogs unlucky not to have a 2–0 lead in their pocket as they return home for the next 3 games in this October classic now tiptoeing into November. I can't cheer for the Rangers for political or even sporting reasons, and I have no love for the Diamondbacks as they dumped my beloved LA Dodgers from the play-offs. Oh the fickle fortunes of watching sport! One wonders what Dave *"Doc"* Roberts, manager of the big spending Dodgers, thinks of it all. Another huge opportunity missed perhaps or does he just lament at the strange and unique nature of watching sport like the rest of us?

Leaving aside pointless rhetorical questions such as these we'll return briefly to the World Cup, and for a cricket competition crying out for a tense, close game, we had two in consecutive days and I had the very real pleasure of watching them both.

South Africa's 1 wicket win against Pakistan has almost certainly assured them of a Semi-Final place and for the losers Pakistan, they have the prospect of a *"dead rubber"* game with England that regardless of the outcome will see them outside of the top 4 Semi-Final spots. It wasn't supposed to be this way for a Pakistan team I tipped as second favourites for the tournament but their defeat to South Africa was perfectly in keeping with their World Cup fortunes. On their way to setting South Africa 271 runs to win, Pakistan batted well, led by their elegant and joy to watch of a captain Babar Azam but he, like Saud Shakeel and Shadam Khan, each posted at least 40 runs but nothing more substantial than 50. Mohammed Rizwan was one of three batsmen to climb into their 20's or 30's, get a firm start, then lose their wickets rather than scoring a big, match changing score. Rizwan in particular was dropped first ball before aggressively embroiling himself in a mid-wicket spat with South African fast bowler Marco Jansen. A pleasing verbal joust of cricketing days past! Jansen would have his revenge with 3 wickets for 43 runs conceded before crashing a quick 20 runs with the bat as his team inched ever nearer their target whilst quixotically, Pakistan neared victory themselves too. The fall of Jansen's wicket was soon followed by that of one of South Africa's many stand out performers of the tournament so far Aiden Markram for a run-a-ball 91.

At 250–7, South Africa needed 21 runs for victory and Pakistan, 3 wickets. Each team edged nervously nearer their target before Tabraiz Shamsi, custodian of 4 Pakistan wickets with his left arm spinning deliveries earlier, struck a boundary 4 for victory and a 1 wicket win.

5 runs was the tiny margin of victory in the following day's battle between neighbours Australia and New Zealand, quite the feat considering the two teams smashed and crashed a combined 65 boundary 4's and 32 boundary clearing 6's on their way to a record combined runs score of 771. Despite my favourite Australian fighting alley-cat David Warner and the returning Travis Head notching an opening stand of 175 and Glenn Maxwell, Josh Inglis and Pat Cummins combing for 116 late innings run, 388 was only 5 runs too many for a New Zealand team destined for the Semi-Finals and a match for anyone in their path.

Rachin Ravindra scored another remarkable century and ultimately 116 from just 89 balls received. Daryl Mitchell looked in imperious touch as always on his way to a run-a-ball 54 and the chasing *"Black Caps"* of New Zealand were in the game, and the chase, until the final ball of the game and the dismissal of James Neesham for a bludgeoning 58 from 39 balls received.

As at the time of writing, Afghanistan are chasing 110 runs from 22 overs to beat Sri Lanka (come on Afghanistan!), the winner will end the day in 5th place in the table behind the top 4 of India, South Africa, New Zealand and Australia and the must be Semi-Finalists come two weeks time, and England are bottom with only a victory over Bangladesh to their name in a World Cup that can't end soon enough for them.

Australia hammer final nail into England's World Cup coffin

Australia v England, 4th November 2023

AUSTRALIA 286 all out
ENGLAND 253 all out

Australia win by 33 runs

With today being *"Super Saturday"* at the World Cup and being the mad dog Englishman that I am, I rose like a lion from my slumbers at 4.45am for a 5am start and the first of two games that saw records set, broken and tumble on a day that was anything but super for the vanquished, dishevelled lions of England and the unlucky Kiwis of New Zealand. Whilst New Zealand put Pakistan to the sword in Bengaluru, scoring their highest ever World Cup score of 401–6 in the process, England captain Jos Buttler won the toss in Ahmedabad and after inserting the auld enemy of Australia into bat,
continued a pattern of their World Cup hence far by having an impressive opening hour and restricting Australia to 38–2 at the fall of the wicket of the dangerous David Warner.

A 75 run partnership followed from the *"Chuckle Brothers"* of Steve Smith and Marnus Labuschagne and together with substantial scores of 47 from Cameron Green, a run-a-ball 35 from Marcus Stoinis and 29 from just 19 balls received from eventual *"Man of the Match"* Adam Zampa, Australia set England 287 for victory. With the ball, Adil Rashid impressed once more for England with 2 wickets for just 38 runs conceded, Mark Wood grabbed 2 wickets for a far more costly 70 runs but pleasingly there was a real return to form for the under-performing Chris Woakes who finished with bowling figures of 4–54.

At the half-way stage England were well and truly in the game.

Returning to Bengaluru, New Zealand captain Kane Williamson continued an impressive return to the team following his brilliant 95 runs from just 79 balls received with the bat with a spectacular running and diving catch to dismiss Abdullah Shafique for just 4 and at 6–1, Pakistan were seemingly about to follow their somewhat traditional pattern of flattering to deceive before their eventual cricketing demise. Chasing 402 to win was imposing enough without their own self-styled ability to implode on the biggest stage, but they'd been backed into a corner by the record breaking Rachin Ravindra with his third century in his debut World Cup and a stunning 108 from just 94 balls received.

Cornered into a near impossible position or not, Pakistan captain Babar Azam knocked a remarkably assured run-a-ball 66 runs in double quick time but this paled in comparison to his teammate at the other end, Fakhar Zaman. The 33 year old returning veteran, having previously been dropped or left out of the starting XI earlier in the tournament, began *"clubbing it, absolutely clubbing it"* according to Pakistan legend Waqar Younis on TV commentary duties before Matthew Hayden, ex Australian batsman who sure could hit a cricket ball a mighty long way in his heyday, described Fakhar Zaman as *"monstering"* the bowling of New Zealand to the furthest reaches of Bengaluru on his way to a stunning half century from 39 balls before reaching his century from just a further 24 balls received.

Whether it was Matthew Hayden's made up word of *"monstering"* (It's Matthew Hayden, he's allowed to make up words!) or more grammatically correct clubbing, Fakhar Zaman crashed and smashed 11 enormous boundary clearing 6's and 8 boundary 4's on his way to 126 from just 81 balls received and at 200–1 from 25 overs, Pakistan were halfway towards an incredible victory.

Then the rain came for a second and final time in their innings and being 21 runs ahead on the *"Duckworth/Lewis Method"* (a cricketing method of determining a victor in the event of bad weather and which will take me a thousand years to explain to you and we'll both be none the wiser), Pakistan had their victory, New Zealand an unfortunate defeat, and both teams now reside in the World Cup table on the cusp of qualification for the Semi-Finals in 4th and 5th positions with only one final spot in the top 4 up for grabs in the coming final week of the Group Stage.

Whilst the rain continued to fall in Bengaluru, England were making the worst possible start to their run chase in Ahmedabad with Jonny Bairstow dismissed with the first ball of their innings and 26 balls later fellow Yorkshireman Joe Root followed him back to the Pavilion and England were already deep in the mire at 19–2. Spirited partnerships between Dawid Malan and Ben Stokes (84) and Stokes and Moeen Ali (63) resurrected English hopes of an improbable victory but despite a returning to form Chris Woakes and his run-a-ball 32 late in the innings, England still fell 33 runs short of their target to remain rooted, embarrassingly, to the foot of the World Cup table below tournament minnows the Netherlands and Bangladesh. Meanwhile their oldest cricketing foes Australia have finally found some form and look nailed on for a Semi-Final spot with 5 wins, 10 points and a current position of 3rd in the table.

Since we were last together, the Texas Rangers finally secured their first World Series title in baseball's *"Big Dance"* defeating a thoroughly outplayed Arizona Diamondbacks, Tyson Fury defeated Francis Ngannou in Saudi Arabia in the biggest boxing *"fix"* since the last one, with the entire event bringing shame on an already heavily tainted sport, and my Mighty Reds of Liverpool continue on their winning ways in a season of transition and evolution under their lovable German manager with the most beautiful of beards, Jürgen Klopp.

Returning to the World Cup in India, the hosts continue to look unbeatable. After disposing with England by 100 runs they demolished a poor Sri Lanka by an almighty 302 runs after bowling them all out for a paltry 55 and at the time of writing are 3 wickets away from thoroughly dismantling South Africa by over 200 runs.

Today's opponents South Africa appear to be the only team to threaten their eventual crowning as World Champions come the Semi-Finals and Final in 2 weeks time and today crowd darling Virat Kohli scored an unbeaten century to match the achievements of national icon Sachin Tendulkar, and on his birthday too!

Nearest and fiercest neighbours Pakistan not only remain in contention due to today's rain affected victory over New Zealand but their 7 wicket win over Bangladesh earlier in the week was notable for yet more records for talismanic fast bowler Shaheen Afridi (100 wickets in One Day Internationals) and yet another bludgeoning and *"monster"* innings from Fakhar Zaman who crashed a quick fire 81 from 74 balls received.

I, on the other hand, remain firmly in the cricketing corner of Afghanistan who since we were last together, brilliantly and thoroughly defeated both Sri Lanka and the Netherlands by 7 wickets on each occasion. I can't help but pull for the spinning twins of Mohammad Nabi and Rashid Khan and the batting expertise of their captain Hashmatullah Shahidi and Rahmat Shah, both of whom scored bags of runs in the respective wins over Sri Lanka and the Netherlands. Afghanistan still need a minor miracle to qualify for the Semi-Finals with their final 2 Group games pitting them against Australia and South Africa with Tuesday's game against the Aussies make or break in their bid for an unbelievable spot at the very top table of world cricket. I'll be cheering them on come Tuesday and should they shake up the world once more they might, just might, dump a tournament favourite such as Pakistan or New Zealand or even Australia from the top 4 and an early exit.

Now that's a sporting story I can get behind!

Maxwell breaks Afghan hearts with an innings for the ages

Netherlands v England, 8th November 2023

ENGLAND 339–9
NETHERLANDS 179 all out

England win by 160 runs

In football parlance, or any sporting vernacular come to that, England's clash with the Netherlands today was a *"bottom of the table"* affair as well as a *"must win game"* for the defending Champions and current holders of the World Cup. A defeat for England would almost certainly guarantee an already embarrassing early exit from the World Cup together with rock bottom status in the Group Stage of 10 teams as well as an equally embarrassing failure to qualify for next year's Champions Trophy in Pakistan. They were therefore indebted to a sparkling century from Test Match captain Ben Stokes and a top and tail of their batting innings saved by 87 from opening batsman Dawid Malan and a run-a-ball half century from Chris Woakes in a late innings partnership with Stokes as the rest of their teammates weakly surrendered their wickets mid-innings.

From 133–1 the heavy favourites collapsed to 192–6 and appeared on the verge of failing to even post 250 when 350 was the absolute bare minimum against the tournament's rank outsiders, but step forward Stokes and Woakes, and 339–9 was always going to be far, far too many for the Netherlands to chase for victory.

At 13–2 it appeared as though the Netherlands would crumble to an even earlier defeat than they finally succumbed to, but battling innings' from Wesley Baresi (37) at the top of the order together with stoic mid-innings stints from Sybrand Engelbrecht (33) and captain Scott Edwards (38) ensured their team passed 100 before a rear guard 41 not out from Teja Nidamanuru tiptoed their innings total to 179 and an expected, if ultimately heavy defeat, by 160 runs. Only Gus Atkinson failed to grab a wicket for England with the ball with spinners Moeen Ali and Adil Rashid, England's top performer with the ball all tournament, shared 6 of the wickets to fall with England's victory leapfrogging them above the Netherlands, Bangladesh and a poor Sri Lanka into 7th place in the World Cup table and although Saturday's final game with Pakistan is still the deadest of dead rubbers (where it should have been a battle for final position in the top 4 and their respective Semi-Final spots), they are now almost certainly assured of a spot in the Champions Trophy next year.

This World Cup still cannot end quickly enough for a poor England team who have under-performed exceedingly badly and with only 2 victories against the tournament minnows Bangladesh and the Netherlands to their name against 6 heavy defeats, their ODI (One Day International) team will limp home to lick their wounds before wholesale changes to an aged squad who ventured one tournament too far.

The same cannot be said for the gallant and infectious enthusiasm of an Afghanistan team who were, against every possible conceivable stack of gambling odds, 6 wickets away from defeating Australia, taking their points tally to 10, their World Cup wins to an incredible 5 and still an outside chance of a Semi-Final berth and a top 4 shoot-out with hosts India.

Then along came Glenn Maxwell who not only played the greatest ODI innings of all time but arguably one of the greatest innings ever seen in the entire history of this storied game, breaking both my sporting heart and that of Afghanistan in the process.

Setting Australia 292 runs to win was a complete team effort from Afghanistan with every batsman reaching sizeable double figure scores as they accompanied opening batsman Ibrahim Zadran who batted the entire 50 overs for an astounding 129 not out from 143 balls received.

He inched his way through the 70's, 80's and 90's with singles before exploding with boundary 6's after becoming Afghanistan's first ever World Cup centurion and with some incredible lusty blows late on from Rashid Khan (35 from 18 balls received), Afghanistan had not only set Australia a competitive total to chase but an exceedingly difficult one too.

At 49–4 Australia were toppling and at 91–7 they were a distant 202 runs away from an almost impossible mission with Afghanistan now just 3 wickets away from arguably their greatest and most important victory in their short history of international cricket.

With victory and an unbelievable spot in the Semi-Finals of the World Cup and at cricket's very top table to boot they faltered, fielding errors began to creep into their play and with Glenn Maxwell on 33 not out he was granted his third and last cricketing *"life"* with the simplest chances at short fine leg a *"dolly"* that was easier to drop than to pouch.

An exhausted Maxwell said immediately after the game that this was the signal that he simply had to go for the victory now, he'd been granted yet another reprieve and two cramp filled, sweat drenched hours later, he broke Afghan hearts with the most incredible innings I've ever witnessed.

From 33 not out Maxwell, in league with his captain Pat Cummins who simply stood at the other end and couldn't hide both his admiration and his smiles as wide as the Sydney Harbour Bridge, raced to a run-a-ball 50, 100 from 76 balls received, 150 from 104 balls received before hobbling on one leg with cramp seizing his leg muscles as to be almost immobile he simply stood and delivered, crashing boundary 4's and 6's to all parts of the Wankhede Stadium. Cummins contributed just 12 of their 202 run partnership as Maxwell hobbled, collapsed to the ground through cramp and exhaustion multiple times, giving rise to ex Australian opening batsman Matthew Hayden to exclaim *"he doesn't know which leg to stand on!"* before clubbing 6, 6, 4 and a final game winning 6 on his way to an EXTRAORDINARY 201 not out from just 128 balls received. Words simply cannot do justice to what I and the rest of the watching world witnessed and all I can conclude with is that I've watched cricket for over 4 decades now and I've never seen the grand old game played in this manner and doubt I ever will again.

Since we were last together, as well as Glenn Maxwell breaking Afghan hearts and thus ensuring his Australia team qualified for the Semi-Finals, New Zealand will almost certainly join them in the 4th and final table position even in spite of their unlucky defeat to Pakistan who will need to heavily defeat England in their final Group game and hope against cricketing hope.

India retained their perfect 100% record as they smashed South Africa by a whopping 243 runs and pleasingly Bangladesh defeated a poor Sri Lanka by 3 wickets on a day when veteran Angelo Mathews was *"timed out"* in cricket's most unusual of all dismissals. Adjusting a faulty batting helmet and not being ready to face a delivery after the specified 2 minutes, he returned to the Pavilion without facing a ball in this most extraordinary of World Cup's where hearts are being broken, double centuries are being clubbed, eyes being deceived, and a host nation will smash the Netherlands on Sunday for a perfect 9 wins from 9 in the Group stage before the Semi-Finals start next Wednesday.

India are nailed on certainties to win this World Cup, they have been from the very start and with a perfect 100% record entering the Semi-Finals are surely expectant ahead of their coronation in 10 days time.

But this is fast becoming a quite extraordinary World Cup and I make no apology for using that word again and whilst Australia have Glenn Maxwell, New Zealand have Rachin Ravindra and South Africa have Quinton de Kock, any and everything is still possible in this fascinating sporting spectacle on the other side of the cricketing world.

The Afghan dream is over

Pakistan v England, 11th November 2023

ENGLAND 337–9

PAKISTAN 244 all out

England win by 93 runs

With one day remaining of the Group stages and tomorrow's expected annihilation of the Netherlands by the unstoppable force that is the host nation India, today was another *"Super Saturday"* in the 2023 Cricket World Cup and whilst Australia cantered past Bangladesh by 8 wickets in Pune, over a thousand miles away in Kolkata two of the tournaments expected Semi-Finalists limped out in the very dictionary definition of a sporting *"dead rubber"*. Pakistan needed a miracle of beyond biblical proportions to advance into the last 4 and as soon as England captain Jos Buttler won the toss and opted to bat first the jig was up, and England finally cashed in on a dominating first hour of play to set up a batting performance absent without leave throughout the entire tournament.

338 to win on this tricky two paced Eden Gardens wicket was always going to be an unrealistic target for Babar Azam and his Pakistan team and as the nighttime mist enveloped this storied sporting venue, they came up a creditable, if defeated, 93 runs short.

My Saturday of super sport was split in two as I watched the England innings before listening to Pakistan's futile run chase on the radio. For perhaps the only occasion in this World Cup England's *"top order"* of 6 batsmen all made significant double figure scores. Book-ended by Dawid Malan's 31 and Harry Brook's quickfire 30 from just 17 balls, Jonny Bairstow finally hit some form on his way to a run-a-ball half century whilst his Yorkshire teammate Joe Root did likewise as he topped and tailed his World Cup with impressive half centuries in an otherwise underwhelming overall tournament with the bat. Captain Jos Buttler rattled a quick 27 before being run out chasing further swift late innings runs and Ben Stokes top scored for the second match running with 84 from just 76 balls received.

Setting Pakistan north of 330 runs to win begs the obvious question:

Where has this performance been hiding for the past few weeks?

But then again, a similar question could be posed to a Pakistan team expected, as were England, to figure in next week's Semi-Finals rather than limping to an unconvincing final position of 5th in the table and in all honesty, a long way short of the top 4.

Listening to the British radio institution of *"Test Match Special"* for the Pakistan run chase was its usual surreal joy as tall tales were weaved and spun like a Shane Warne leg-break of hitchhiking with a passer-by to make an important bus trip, 36 hour train journeys across India with a travelling astrologer for company and the all important preparations in place for tomorrow's Diwali festival. A picture was brilliantly painted of numerous gatherings, home cooked food and card games as a mist shrouded a cricket ground I've long held high in my cricketing admiration before we had the bizarre description of a broken *"Zinger"* bail, boxes of replacements and a host of technicians all seemingly endeavouring to ensure this 21st Century technology adhered to a 19th Century pastime that has recorded roots in a cricketing century or two even before that.

All of which made for an entertaining listen as Pakistan lost their first wicket with the second delivery of their innings, were 10–2 in double quick time and 61–3 at the fall of their captain Babar Azam for 38.

The Pakistan innings then became a tale of two halves as their middle order of Mohammad Rizwan, Saud Shakeel and Salman Agha all scored 30+ runs in a spirited resistance before an even arguably more impressive refusal to collapse to defeat was demonstrated by some lusty late order blows from Shaheen Afridi with a run-a-ball 25, Mohammad Wasim with a similarly run-a-ball 16 and especially Haris Rauf with 35 from just 23 balls received. Rauf was the last man out giving Chris Woakes his only wicket of the innings but ensuring that every England bowler snagged a Pakistan batting victim as Adil Rashid, Gus Atkinson and Moeen Ali all grabbed 2 wickets apiece and *"Man of the Match"* David Willey, the only England player not to be offered a central contract for the coming seasons, finishing with bowling figures of 3–56.

England's underwhelming World Cup therefore ended with the irony of a star *"Man of the Match"* performance from the only player deemed surplus to future requirements.

It rather summed up their defence of a World Cup they'll be looking to forget in a hurry.

Since we were last together, alas the Afghanistan World Cup dream has died. Following their heart breaking defeat to Australia on Tuesday and lest we forget, only as a result of one of THE innings of all time from Glenn Maxwell, they tumbled to a 5 wicket defeat to South Africa yesterday in yet another game they were highly competitive in, if coming up agonisingly short once more. It was always going to be the tallest of orders to vanquish both of these ultimate Semi-Finalists but boy did they run them both close! They will end this World Cup in 6th position and just one win away from the top table and should be lauded to the skies for their mighty achievement in the process.

New Zealand have ultimately pipped them to the post and the 4th and final Semi-Final spot, thus setting up the unenviable prospect of a 50 over cricketing battle with hosts India on Wednesday for a berth in Sunday's Final against the winners of the other Semi-Final between an in form Australia and an impressive South Africa.

New Zealand are plagued with injuries.

India look unbeatable.

I'd written off Australia before the tournament began.

And South Africa so often fall at the final hurdle.

I can't see past an India/South Africa Final and ultimate glory for the home nation but then again, I'd dismissed Australia as a team in transition and a tournament too early and New Zealand have made the last two World Cup Finals!

We have 3 mouth watering games to look forward to and I for one cannot wait.

Kohli and Shami guide India to one win from destiny

India v New Zealand, 15th November 2023

INDIA 397–4
NEW ZEALAND 327 all out

India win by 70 runs

At 220–2 with skipper Kane Williamson 69 not out and teammate Daryl Mitchell on the precipice of a third stunning century in this pulsating Semi-Final in Mumbai, the *"Black Caps"* of New Zealand were still a distant 178 runs from victory but, rather improbably, still in with a fighting chance of reaching their third cricket World Cup Final in a row. Indian skipper Rohit Sharma, so dominant this morning with the bat as he set both the tone and a platform for his team's innings and the centuries from Virat Kohli and Shreyas Iyer that followed, threw the ball once more to his magic man Mohammed Shami and 4 deliveries later, he'd removed the out of form Tom Latham for a 2 ball *"duck"* who followed his skipper Williamson back to the Pavilion in quick order and 220–2 swiftly became 220–4, Shami had all 4 wickets to fall and New Zealand's fighting chance soon dwindled to a faint hope of a cricketing miracle.

That miracle fell squarely upon the shoulders of Daryl Mitchell who did indeed complete a quite incredible century from just 85 balls received after having rattled a quick fire 50 from just 49 balls received to stabilise the Kiwis innings in tandem with his skipper Kane Williamson. With both Devon Conway and Rachin Ravindra snagged cheaply by Shami and New Zealand 39-2, 398 for victory was a long shot in anyone's cricket score book but Williamson and Mitchell rebuilt the innings to the point of securing rather shorter odds for victory than a sporting miracle. But back came Shami once more and with the game as good as over, grabbed the vital wicket of a cramping and exhausted Daryl Mitchell for a heroic 134 from just 119 balls before taking the wickets of tail-enders Tim Southee and Lockie Ferguson for good measure, and the 33 year old veteran from Amroha finished with the otherworldly bowling figures of 7-57. In a World Cup Semi-Final!

That New Zealand came so close and made a real competitive game of this Semi-Final is to their eternal credit but, and it's a big but, they rather played a part in their own downfall earlier in the day. Spin bowlers Mitchell Santner and Glenn Phillips aside, every other bowler in their attack came in for some fearful punishment and whilst it wasn't always self inflicted with wayward or ill disciplined bowling, when it arrived, it was pounced upon by an eager Indian batting unit roared on by an incredible partisan crowd.

One of life's final untainted indulgences is watching Rohit Sharma bat and his swashbuckling 47 from just 29 balls received was both a true joy to behold as well as setting the table for the batting assault that followed. Opening partner Shubman Gill played second fiddle as his captain plundered quick runs before grasping the mantle himself with a half century from 41 balls before retiring hurt mid-way through the innings with what seemed like cramp. He returned later in the innings to finish 80 not out but not before replacement Shreyas Iyer crashed a 67 ball century and KL Rahul a quick fire 39 from 20 balls as India rattled up a virtually unbeatable 397–4.

Which leaves us with crowd darling Virat Kohli, the *"glue"* of the innings once more and with the Mumbai crowd constantly chanting *"Kohli, Kohli, Kohli"*, their darling delivered a 106 ball century on his way to a final total of 117. Leaving the field to deafening cheers all around him, the 35 year old from New Delhi waved to every corner of the Wankhede Stadium before blowing his wife a kiss and bowing in deference to Sachin Tendulkar in the crowd.

The *"Little Master"* couldn't hide his delight or admiration for Kohli even though he'd surpassed his seemingly unbeatable record of 49 One Day International centuries. He had, on home turf too, and in a World Cup Semi-Final to boot!

I can't hide my admiration for the batting excellence of Rohit Sharma or Virat Kohli or indeed the superlative bowling skills of Jasprit Bumrah or Mohammed Shami, but this Indian team are so overwhelming favourites I can't cheer for them in the Final on Sunday.

Whether Australia or South Africa triumph in tomorrow's Semi-Final in Kolkata I can't see either team denying this incredible India team from becoming World Champions or from what they've shown the world they are these past seven weeks, a team of destiny.

Captain Cummins leads Australia into World Cup Final

Australia v South Africa, 16th November 2023

SOUTH AFRICA 212 all out
AUSTRALIA 215-7

Australia win by 3 wickets

Prologue: *A captain's tale*

When South African captain Temba Bavuma won the toss and elected to bat first it was universally agreed amongst an excitable TV commentary team that he'd made the correct call even in spite of the heavy rain filled clouds above Eden Gardens, the muggy conditions conducive to fast swing bowling and a wicket that will have sweated beneath the covers protecting it from the overnight rain showers. Post-match, Australian captain Pat Cummins admitted he wasn't unhappy to have lost the toss and, in the vernacular of this grandest of all games, it was a *"good toss to lose"*.

But that's getting ahead of ourselves.

Opening the innings for South Africa, Bavuma would last just 4 balls before *"nicking off"* to a swinging delivery from Mitchell Starc into the waiting gloves of wicket-keeper Josh Inglis and just 28 stupendous fast swinging deliveries later from Starc and bowling partner Josh Hazlewood, Quinton de Kock, playing in his final One Day International for his country and upon whose shoulders much of the success of their innings rested, skied a difficult chance high into a gloomy Kolkata afternoon sky. Tracking the ball and running backwards and sideways was Aussie captain Pat Cummins. Safely pouching the catch before falling backwards onto the ground, Cummins released a guttural roar of delight, South Africa were already toppling at 8–2 which soon became 24–4 and Australia were in complete control of a Semi-Final they'd eventually win, but not without a scare or two along the way.

Epilogue: A captain's tale

Temba Bavuma was incredibly magnanimous in defeat as he congratulated Australia in their *"thoroughly deserved win"* after a *"good display of cricket"*. He admitted his team were always *"playing catch up"* after such a poor start with the bat and reserved the highest of praise for Quinton de Kock as a *"legend of the game"*, for David Miller's incredible century epitomising and *"speaking to the character of our team"* and finally 23 year old Gerald Coetzee, a late inclusion to the team and squad and quite simply a *"warrior"*.

Despite the heartbreak of coming so close once more in a World Cup Semi-Final, Bavuma spoke with such grace and generosity.

Victorious captain Pat Cummins, yet again at the business end of an incredible game of cricket but not with his speciality as the number one rated bowler in Test Match cricket but with the bat, couldn't hide his delight at being *"pumped"* by the win and that he'd emerged from a *"very happy changing room"*. He admitted the run chase had ended in a *"nervy couple of hours"* but preferred being in the middle of the cricketing battle rather than watching on from the sidelines, as he was this evening, with Glenn Maxwell too for his never to be forgotten double century against Afghanistan and particularly this Summer to break English hearts at Edgbaston in The Ashes. He rightly acclaimed Mitchell Starc and Josh Hazlewood as *"ridiculous"* with their opening spell of fast bowling before confirming the obvious and self-evident. It may well be an incredible eighth World Cup Final for his country and the support on Sunday will be, said with a mighty laugh, *"one-sided"*, but they'll *"embrace"* the occasion and *"enjoy it"* come what may.

If you were to take a peek within the pages of my two self-published books available via www.amazon.com *"Ashes to Ashes"* and *"The Spirit of Cricket"* you'll notice a tongue in cheek pattern emerge whereby I constantly question whether in fact Pat Cummins is the real captain of Australia.

Steve Smith, now fully rehabilitated following the outrageous cheating scandal surrounding *"Sandpapergate"* always seems to me to be the on-field captain and I ended this Summer's book poking fun at the prospect of Pat Cummins returning to Australia under a cloud of uncertainty despite leading his country to World Test Champions and holders of The Ashes. I suggested Steve Smith will be forever hovering in the wings waiting to take over the captaincy and/or an Australian Cricket Board wanting him to be captain if only to ensure he continues donning the *"Baggy Green"*, postponing talk of retirement, and taking to the cricket field to represent his country. Even as an English *"Pom"*, I will be as pleased as anyone to see Pat Cummins leading his team in the unenviable quest to defeat the unbeatable looking India on their home turf this coming Sunday.

In between these captain's tales came an extraordinary South African batting collapse, a bowling spell from Josh Hazlewood from the cricketing Gods and an innings saving century of guts, guile and gusto from David Miller without which South Africa would have slumped to an early and ignominious defeat. Hazlewood, consistently and brilliantly bowling into an *"ice cream bucket"* according to the excitable analysis of ex Australian opening batsman Matthew Hayden, finished with the astonishing figures of 2–12 but with his partner in crime Mitchell Starc ripped the heart out of the top order of the South African innings.

Heinrich Klaasen and Gerald Coetzee kept David Miller company for his innings saving century and from a tottering 44–4 at a rain break, South Africa admirably posted a still light but competitive final total of 212 all out.

Travis Head cemented his *"Man of the Match"* performance both with bat and ball as he firstly snagged the vital wickets of Heinrich Klaasen and Marco Jansen in consecutive spinning deliveries before dispatching Jansen and his fellow South African fast bowlers to all parts of Eden Gardens on his way to a 40 ball half century and eventual table setting innings of 62 from just 48 balls received. From 106–2 at the fall of Head's wicket, Australia chipped away at the remaining 106 runs needed for victory all the while losing wickets at regular intervals and at the fall of the dangerous Glenn Maxwell for just 1 they still needed 75 runs to win. Step forward a priceless knock of 30 from Steve Smith, 28 from Josh Inglis and with 20 still needed for victory and a place in the World Cup Final, it was their captain Pat Cummins, one of the greatest bowlers in the world in any form of this great game, who guided them home once more with the bat.

So it's onto the Narendra Modi Stadium in Ahmedabad on Sunday for the World Cup Final and the showdown between an Australian team in their eighth Final and as usual, peaking at the right time, and an Indian team with destiny in their cricketing sights.

With well in excess of 100,000 expected in this vast sporting coliseum there will be the tiniest smattering of Australian green and gold surrounded on all sides by the blue of India for a game that really and truly only has one conceivable winner.

But you write off Australia at your own peril.

Just as I did even before the tournament started seven long weeks ago!

Australia spoil the Indian coronation to become World Champions

World Cup Final

India v Australia, 19th November 2023

INDIA 240 all out
AUSTRALIA 241-4

Australia win by 6 wickets

When Australian captain Pat Cummins won the pre-game toss and inserted India into bat it was a ballsy move to say the very least. Contravening time held cricketing traditions and inviting your opposition to bat first, in a World Cup Final no less as well as a team looking unbeatable after winning ten straight games out of ten and on home soil backed by a vociferous Ahmedabad crowd of way over 100,000 was not only audacious, against the long held perceived wisdom of this grandest of all games but unconventional and fraught with repercussions and recriminations should the skipper's decision backfire.

But this Australian team, led by the 30 year old fast bowler from Westmead in Sydney, are anything but conventional.

There have been bizarre injuries inflicted away from the cricket field, a death in the immediate family of one of their prized all-rounders and as the team and larger squad scraped their way back into the World Cup after losing their opening two games they faced almost certain elimination or a tougher Semi-Final spot against today's opponents when their freewheeling talisman dragged them off the canvas against Afghanistan with a double century for the ages and an innings that will defy your lying eyes forever more. Throw in a batsman completely out of form, a 37 year old fighting alley cat who tore around the outfield akin to a man half his age, veteran bowlers who were surely venturing into the cliched territory of playing *"one tournament too many"*, a batsman considered too slow and ponderous to play this shorter form of the game and an opening batsman who missed the beginning of the tournament as he recovered from a fractured hand, and you can see why I had reasons for doubting this Australian team, and not after their opening two defeats but pre-tournament too. I wrote off the chances of this Australian team as I felt they were a team in transition and between the ending of a once great team and the building of their next one.

After watching the nucleus of this team, and a team that has been a larger squad of 14/15 players since way before the 2021 Ashes Series with England, you'd think I'd know better and that I shouldn't have rushed to judgement.

Please don't mistake my discounting of their World Cup chances for misplaced patriotism for my home country or any bitterness regarding their two recent tussles for the safekeeping of The Ashes. I'm a huge admirer of the batting prowess of David Warner and Marnus Labuschagne as well as the incredible bowling skills of their trio of fast bowling greats Pat Cummins, Josh Hazlewood and Mitchell Starc. My self-published books *"Ashes to Ashes"* and *"The Spirit of Cricket"* are testament to this. I watch cricket objectively, obsessively and for the love of this grandest of all games and in the spirit of my parents who introduced me to the wonders of leather on willow over four decades ago. I just saw a team that was past its peak and on the downward curve before their inevitable rise once more and how wrong could I be!

Today the World Test Champions and custodians of that precious urn of cricketing ashes became World Cup winners for the sixth time, and that 37 year old fighting alley cat from Paddington near Sydney raced around the outfield once more saving vital runs, Cummins, Hazlewood and Starc snagged seven Indian wickets between them and, when on the cusp of severe trouble at 47-3 and over 100,000 partisan Indian cricket fans baying for more Australian sporting blood, step forward the man who many (but not me) didn't feel merited a place in the team and an opening batsman recently recovered from a fractured hand and a near 200 run partnership later, the World Cup was Australian green and gold once more.

You really shouldn't write off an Australian cricket team and especially one as unconventional as this one.

So what of the runaway train that was India, the champions elect on their home turf and the team seemingly racing to their sporting destiny after a perfect ten wins from ten on their way to the Final? One can't help but feel incredible sadness and empathy for a nation who regard this wonderful old game as a near religious event and for their captain Rohit Sharma whom I simply adore watching wield a cricketing willow. England tour India for a five Test Match series in early 2024 and I cannot wait to see battle recommence in cricketing whites rather than the coloured clothing and *"pajamas"* as so sweetly described by my cricket loving mother. Shubman Gill is yet another wunderkind from their cricket production line with a hugely successful career ahead of him. Crowd darling Virat Kohli scored yet another half-century today to top the run scoring charts for this tournament and later accorded, in the most bittersweet way on a day of deep disappointment, *"Man of the Tournament"*. Mohammed Shami ended as the tournament's top wicket taker. KL Rahul notched an invaluable 66 and spin bowlers Ravindra Jadeja and Kuldeep Yadav had impressive, if ultimately unsuccessful, World Cups. Led by Rohit Sharma and the seemingly ageless Virat Kohli, all of these Indian cricketing heroes will be gunning for England come the earliest of months next year.

But to the victors go the spoils.

Yet another *"Man of the Match"* display from Travis Head to add to his Semi-Final accolade of three days ago and his always impressive showings in Ashes battles with England. Described as a *"Legend"* by Australian captain Pat Cummins post-match, he also rightly acclaimed his entire team's approach today as *"Brave"* and *"You have to be brave to win a World Cup"* before confirming they'd peaked at the right time and *"This is a year we will remember for a long, long time"*.

World Test Champions.

Holders of The Ashes.

World Cup Winners.

A year to remember indeed! I heralded today's performance on Twitter as arguably one of if not THE greatest *"Away"* wins in all sports.

But what else should I have expected from this unconventional team for the ages?

Part Two: Winter tour to India, 2024

Jimmy joins the "700 Club" as India unearth a possible team for the ages

India in the box seat after day 1 in Hyderabad

Thursday 25th January, 2024

ENGLAND 246 all out
INDIA 119-1 *(trail by 127)*

It was long past the witching hour of midnight when, after penning my songs of written praise for my beloved Reds of Liverpool Football Club reaching the first Wembley cup final of the English football season, that I retreated to bed beneath the fullest and brightest of moons and eagerly awaiting the first day of England's daunting new year tour of India. Together with the Ashes tours of Australia every four years, India ranks as high on the difficulty scale of being triumphant and a much changed England team were also dealt the twin blows of losing the immediate services of Shoaib Bashir due to visa issues as well as the mightily impressive Harry Brook for undisclosed family issues. Whilst Brook may not return to the tour, Bashir is expected to be available for selection from the second Test Match onward, which cannot be said for Indian crowd darling Virat Kohli who, like Harry Brook, has withdrawn from at least the first two Test Matches and like Brook once more, uncertainty reigns as to whether he will feature in this series at all.

With England much changed, India can also lay a similar claim but home conditions favour them as well as the leadership of their talismanic captain Rohit Sharma and the simple and honest facts that the team by team match-ups favour them considerably. Whilst there may not be much to split the respective opening batting partnerships of Rohit Sharma and Yashasvi Jaiswal for the home side and Zak Crawley and Ben Duckett for the visitors, I fear that if Yorkshire's finest Joe Root and Jonny Bairstow fail with the bat they'll be eclipsed by the Indian middle order of KL Rahul and Shreyas Iyer. But the largest fears of all reside in the huge discrepancy between India's highly experienced and brilliant spin bowling attack of Ravi Jadeja and Ravi Ashwin (aided and abetted by Axar Patel) and England's spin bowling options of Jack Leach, 19 year old Rehan Ahmed, debutant Tom Hartley and the always *"golden arm"* from the part-time spin of Joe Root.

So with less than 90 minutes of restful sleep I awoke at 3.30am for the first time of many in the 7 cricketing weeks that will follow, stretching into early March and the ending of this tour, and a 5 Test Match series in which I do not foresee a drawn match and whilst my heart hopes for a tight and valiant 3–2 series defeat for England, I fear 4–1 or, whisper it, even worse. But irrational hope springs eternal and we have plenty of time ahead for more reasoned sporting realism, and so here is the session by session breakdown of the opening day of this Hyderabad Test Match.

Act One: *"And it all started so well"*

Although in a half asleep, half awake state, I was immediately struck by the paucity in build up from the usually excellent TNT Sports here in the UK. Where normally they have a panel of ex England cricketers both *"in country"* and in a UK studio, now they have nothing more than a distant colour commentary voice and the expected build up was next to non-existent. Being experienced in such matters I therefore turned to the tried and tested Fox Sports of Australia who were rather aptly also showing the first day's play from the second Test Match between their home nation and the touring West Indian team and a series I've also been watching, together with their cricketing tussle with Pakistan, since the turn of the year. I've been rather spoiled by Fox Sports Australia and their superior channel dedication to cricket for some years now and whilst readying myself for the toss from Hyderabad and nestling beneath a warming pile of duvets to beat away the cold of an English winter, I couldn't help but chuckle to myself that I was reliant upon a *"feed"* of the Test Match from the sunshine of an Indian summer from the early afternoon sunshine from Brisbane in Australia, and a Day/Night Test Match that ran exactly concurrently with the morning's action from Hyderabad I was watching at 4am on a bitterly cold English morning and under the fullest and brightest of moons!

So much for all that.

England captain Ben Stokes won the toss and immediately announced his team would have first dibs with the bat, and for 45 or so minutes, the little and large opening partnership of Ben Duckett and Zak Crawley cajoled and caressed a quick fire 50 run partnership from the fast bowling of Jasprit Bumrah and Mohammed Siraj. It was all rather plain sailing and the England innings had started so well and in a bright and breezy, free scoring fashion.

Whilst England never collapsed on their way to an eventual all out total of 246 they did struggle from hereon in and the pattern was set either side of the first hour's drinks break, the losing of wickets in clusters and the establishing of batting partnerships that blossomed but frustratingly never fully bloomed. Ben Duckett fell for an entertaining run-a-ball 35 runs on the cusp of the hourly break before vice-captain Ollie Pope looked badly out of form as he, in the cricketing vernacular, *"scratched around"* before falling to a sharp catch at 1st Slip from Rohit Sharma off the bowling of Ravi Jadeja for just 1 run and from just the 4th ball after the resumption of play. Zak Crawley soon followed for 20 and with his wicket falling to fellow spin bowler Ravi Ashwin, another pattern for the England innings had been set with all 3 wickets falling to the spinning partnership of Jadeja and Ashwin and by the end of the innings, they'd account for 6 of the 10 wickets to fall.

Such matters were for the future at this stage and under the experienced Yorkshire pair of former captain Joe Root (18 not out) and Jonny Bairstow (32 not out), England reached the Lunch Break on 108–3. Honours even after 2 hours of play.

Act Two: *"It's too good. It's too good. It's too good!"*

From 108–3 at Lunch, England retreated in rather poorer shape at the Tea Break at 215–8 and wholly indebted to yet another patient, battling innings from skipper Ben Stokes. Before he rested his bat at the break in play on 43 not out, he'd watched the Yorkshire pair of Bairstow and Root fall quickly in the afternoon session with Bairstow brilliantly bowled by a gem of a spinning delivery from Axar Patel after adding just 5 runs to his pre-Lunch total of 32 and Root adding 11 before playing arguably the only reckless shot of the innings as he swept a spinning delivery from Jadeja into the grateful hands of Jasprit Bumrah. Although both Rehan Ahmed (13) and debutant Tom Hartley (23) would admirably assist Ben Stokes in cameo batting partnerships throughout the afternoon session, the albeit painful highlight fell to Ben Foakes when, on the cusp of the mid-session break for drinks, he was brilliantly dismissed by Axar Patel in a delivery that spun viciously before snagging the edge of his bat and into the hands of wicket-keeper Srikar Bharat that saw ex England captain Kevin Pietersen enthusing on TV commentary *"It's too good. It's too good. It's too good!"*.

It was, and England were teetering on the brink of collapse.

Act Three: *Jaiswal puts England to the sword*

That England didn't collapse was due almost entirely to captain Ben Stokes who took his not out total of 43 pre the Tea Break to a final 70 and in doing so received a cricketing *"life"* straight after the resumption of play, reached his half century with a towering boundary 6 from 69 total balls received before receiving an unplayable delivery from Jasprit Bumrah that pitched around leg stump before jagging viciously off the wicket, pinging back his middle stump and dismantling his *"castle"* of stumps behind him.

Stokes looked in astonishment at both the wicket and at Bumrah before both players shared a wry smile at both the delivery itself and the reaction it received from the wicket, and England, verging on collapse at 155–7, had made an almost par total of 246 all out.

It was still 30 runs short but at least 30 runs more than was feared had Stokes not batted his way to his usual heroics.

With every run now cheered heartily by a Hyderabad crowd who'd grown steadily in attendance throughout the day, captain Rohit Sharma played rather a backseat role to his junior opening partner Yashasvi Jaiswal as the 22 year old scored the vast majority of their dominating first wicket stand of 80 before Sharma, a batsman I greatly admire, *"holed out"* to his opposite number Stokes for a fine running catch off the bowling of Jack Leach. Joined now by Shubman Gill through to the end of play *"stumps"*, whilst Gill helped himself to a comfortable and carefree 13 runs, Jaiswal crashed his way to an end of play total of 76 not out from just 70 balls received and his team to an incredibly commanding overnight total of 119–1 to trail England after day 1 by just 127 runs.

So after an even first session the honours fall fairly and squarely to the hosts after day 1 and I'm already fearing the worst for an England team who battled gamely throughout a tough day, almost made a competitive par score, but are firmly behind on my judge's scorecard. Early wickets tomorrow to restrict India to only parity on their first innings total is crucial as a lead for the home team will see an England victory a distant prospect as batting on days 3 and 4 on this wicket against the likes of Ravi Ashwin and Ravi Jadeja will not be any fun whatsoever!

Time will tell.

It always does.

India forge ahead on "Republic Day"
Friday 26th January, 2024

ENGLAND 246 all out
INDIA 421–1 *(lead by 175 runs)*

It was hard to disagree with ex England captain Eoin Morgan this morning as he excitedly exclaimed *"You will not regret setting your alarm"* and that today's opening session of play would be *"box office"* but then again, it was 3.30am on a cold and frosty Friday morning and in the words of my favourite band Radiohead I think I've got the bends from rising too early, and are England *"really sinking this low"*?

The answers to these rhetorical questions are, in reverse order, yes, yes it was, and no I didn't, even though India were magnificent as they ground England into the cricketing dirt to take an almost unbeatable lead with three full days of play still scheduled.

Naturally the alarm is set for 3.30am tomorrow as quite simply England need to take the final 3 Indian wickets as quickly as possible before their lead climbs above 200 runs and beyond, and they have to dislodge Ravi Jadeja and take the bat from his hand before resisting everything the highly skilled spin bowler has to offer in tandem with his spin bowling partners Ravi Ashwin and Axar Patel on a wearing wicket that is turning, getting lower and slower and perfect for their mesmeric art of spin bowling.

Now that's box office!

Talking of which, here are today's three sessions of play:

Act One: *"Golden Arm" and a costly cricketing "life"*

Starting day 2 on 119–1 and 127 runs behind England's 1st innings total, a huge celebratory bank holiday crowd inside the Rajiv Gandhi International Stadium welcomed yesterday's batting hero Yashasvi Jaiswal back to the wicket and on 76 not out, stood just 24 runs from a Test Match century. The 22 year old from Suriyawan belted the day's second delivery from Joe Root for a boundary 4 as seemingly a statement of intent before trying to repeat the trick two deliveries later, only to see England's part-time spin bowler and cricketing *"Golden Arm"* snaffle a high and sharp return catch to dismiss the young batsman *"Caught and Bowled"* for a brilliantly made 80.

It was quite the start to the day and an even more impressive catch, the day's first over had still yet to be completed, there was still another box office moment on the horizon, and a costly cricketing *"life"* afforded to incoming batsman KL Rahul that has undoubtedly changed the course of this Test Match.

Root's final delivery of the day's first over pitched around off stump before spinning just enough to snag the outside edge of Rahul's bat with the resulting sharp catching chance flying past the gloves of England wicket-keeper Ben Foakes. The post game analysis and podcasts I've listened to suggest it was a catchable chance and not difficult, but I beg to differ. It was quick, sharp and difficult, but a chance nonetheless. Regardless, Rahul had received a cricketing *"life"* and when he was finally dismissed later in the afternoon 86 costly runs had been added to his team's total and England were in deep, deep trouble.

As ever that's getting ahead of ourselves and before this, Rahul accumulated 40 runs by the mid-session break for drinks, a half century from just 72 balls received and remained not out at the Lunch Break on 55 with his team now only trailing England by 24 runs, on a total of 222–3 and with 7 wickets still in hand.

Whilst England grabbed the prized wicket of Shubman Gill for 23, Rahul and new batting partner Shreyas Iyer continued to pile on the runs in an opening session of 103 runs to close in on an England team only really noteworthy for the first Test Match wicket for debutant Tom Hartley who snagged Gill mid-session.

Act Two: *Rahul and Jadeja take Rehan Ahmed "downtown"*

The wonderful world of the grandest of all games is awash in its very own vernacular and phrases and I use them as often as I can. One I rarely use though is *"downtown"* meaning a batsman has *"danced"*, *"waltzed"* or more simply run down the wicket and crashed a bowler straight or near straight back past him and towering into the stands for a boundary 6. Although India lost the wicket of Shreyas Iyer immediately after the Lunch Break, both KL Rahul and Ravi Jadeja decided to break the temporary stranglehold on runs held by England by clubbing spin bowlers Tom Hartley and particularly Rehan Ahmed for repeated huge 6's into an adoring crowd. Thus the minor lead held by England at Lunch disappeared and although KL Rahul was finally out, and to a dreadful *"long hop"* of a delivery that presented Rehan Ahmed a semblance of revenge as well as both an easy catch and a second Test Match wicket for Tom Hartley, Ravi Jadeja continued in his stead to end the session on 45 not out, India 309–5, and an already imposing 1st innings lead of 63 runs with still 5 wickets in hand.

Act Three: *India continue to pile on the misery*

The day's final session was notable for coming full circle and yet another *"life"*, this time afforded Ravi Jadeja who overturned an incorrect LBW umpiring decision when 49 not out, a fully deserved second wicket for England's *"Golden Arm"* of Joe Root as he dismissed wicket-keeper batsman Srikar Bharat for 41, and yet more batting partnerships as India continued to pile on the runs. 112 runs were scored in the session as aside from the comical run out of Ravi Ashwin for just 1, Jadeja partnered Bharat for another 50 runs before ending a dominating day with the bat with his spin bowling partner Axar Patel in sharing an unbeaten stand of 62. Patel ended the day 35 not out and accompanied his senior partner Jadeja as he reached his half century to an enormous roar from the Hyderabad crowd and from just 84 balls received, before ending the day to return tomorrow morning 81 not out.

The ultra positive perspective is that England may wrap up the Indian batting *"tail"* in mere minutes and be a maximum 200 runs adrift on 1st innings.

The more negative outlook?

Ravi Jadeja is just 19 runs from a Test Match century.

Axar Patel is just 15 runs from a Test Match half-century.

And India will no doubt wish to bat on for as long as possible, gain as big a 1st innings lead as possible, and negate any reason whatsoever for batting again on a wearing wicket ripe for the bowling expertise of Jadeja, Patel and their spin bowling partner, Ravi Ashwin.

Frankly, England have their backs to the wall.

The audacity of Pope gives England hope

Saturday 27th January, 2024

ENGLAND 246 and 316-6 *(leading by 126 runs)*
INDIA 436 all out

"When we started today, we didn't know we'd have a tomorrow. Because of Ollie Pope, we have a tomorrow".

So enthused ex England captain Kevin Pietersen at the end of yet another enthralling day of Test Match cricket and another of those beautiful reasons for why I adore this grandest of all games so. I've written extensively on my love for the extended form of this game in my previous two books *"Ashes to Ashes"* and *"The Spirit of Cricket"* and that following the wise guidance of my parents and particularly a much missed Mum who ADORED Test Match cricket, I've been a passionate advocate for the game for over four decades now. It's one of the many reasons why I'm penning these thoughts now, immediately after the end of play, half awake and desperate for the sleep that will evade me anyway, bubbling with endless thoughts on a performance that may, just may, have dragged England into a competitive position after having their backs firmly and desperately to the wall.

Memories of my dear old Mum who was in her element with the day ahead and just a long day of cricket, the crack of leather on willow, stretching out before her. How a team can be so outplayed as to be staring at an almost certain defeat after losing every session of the match so far yet *"win"* two of today's three sessions and from nowhere, they may, just may, have a punchers chance of throwing a knock-out blow tomorrow.

All of which is for the future. For now we must return to the present or indeed the very recent past if you will, and a superlative performance from a 26 year old from Chelsea in London named Ollie Pope, a 19 year old kid from Nottingham, a pugnacious fighter from Bromley in Kent, the unorthodox batting style of a man grasping Test Match cricket by its lapels as he approaches his 30th birthday, the infectious enthusiasm of a fast bowler known universally and affectionately as *"Woody"*, a soon to be legend of the game and ex England captain who started this day so magnificently, and all led by Ben Stokes who seemingly refuses to give up on lost causes.

Even a cause as dire as this one.

Act One: *Positive steps forward from the visitors*

As already alluded to, I ended yesterday's journal stating that England had their backs firmly to the wall and it was easy to see why I'd made such an obvious claim. India resumed this morning on 421–7 and with both a commanding lead of 175 runs on 1st innings and two batsmen, Ravi Jadeja and Axar Patel, 81 and 35 not out respectively and both closing in on their individual batting milestones. Veterans Mark Wood and Joe Root opened the bowling for an England team desperate for early wickets and whilst this wasn't immediately achieved, they bowled tight, stifling overs that saw the Indian batsmen score just 6 runs in the opening 30 minutes of play.

As the day's crowd steadily filed into the Rajiv Gandhi International Stadium, joining England's travelling troop of supporters affectionately known around the world as *"The Barmy Army"*, as it was Saturday and as is tradition, fancy dress was the order of the day for some, with one fine fellow deciding that a day of Test Match cricket in Hyderabad called for him attending dressed as Charlie Chaplin! It was clearly his *"Favourite Pastime"* and there was zero chance of him being *"Caught in the Rain"* in Hyderabad, but shall I continue with films from 110 years ago or shall we just get to the action on the field of play?

India would add just a further 9 total runs this morning in the next 20 minutes of play to be bowled all out for 436 and a commanding lead on 1st innings of 190 runs. Joe Root's *"Golden Arm"* was once more to the fore, snagging the vital wicket of Ravi Jadeja an unlucky 13 runs from a Test Match century before clean bowling Jasprit Bumrah with his next delivery to set up a hat-trick that sadly, never materialised. It was left to 19 year old Rehan Ahmed to repeat the clean bowling trick shortly thereafter on Axar Patel who fell 6 runs short of his half-century, but both batsmen performed magnificently last evening to set up this morning's final all out total and intimidating lead on 1st innings.

The hour and 10 minutes that remained of the opening session was all England once more and only blighted by the dismissal of Zak Crawley for a well played and authoritative run-a-ball 31 and he was only undone by a beautifully spinning delivery from Ravi Ashwin that snagged the edge of his bat and into the celebratory hands of his skipper Rohit Sharma. At 45–1 it was a vital and highly acclaimed first England wicket and with the visitors still trailing by a mammoth 145 runs, India were in the box seat and scenting further wickets before the Lunch Break.

But England added a further 44 runs without alarm or loss of any further wickets to enter the break for lunch on 89–1, with Ben Duckett racing along at a run-a-ball 38 not out and Ollie Pope, looking far more assured and comfortable than his skittish 1st innings batting display, 16 not out.

England trailed India on 1st innings at the break by 101 runs.

Act Two: *"It's Boom Boom Bumrah!"*

Without wishing to over-egg the cricketing pudding, the second session of the day epitomised why I adore this game so. England, fighting their way back into the Test Match and finally winning a session of play, are then rocked back on their heels by a fightback from the home team and a quite scintillating bowling spell from Jasprit Bumrah. The 30 year old from Ahmedabad has a bowling style all of his own and one you'll never find in a coaching manual, but once again he roared in to great effect and, after snagging the prized wickets of Ben Duckett and Joe Root, he quite literally roared!

The next 15 or so minutes was pure sporting theatre and magnificent to witness live albeit, from the other side of the world.

Shortly after the Lunch Break, Bumrah wrapped Ben Duckett on his pads playing back to a vicious swinging delivery and despite pleading with the umpire to give the England batsman out LBW (Leg Before Wicket), he was denied. As he was by his captain Rohit Sharma who refused his plea to refer the decision to DRS (Decision Review System) or more plainly, the TV umpire. Bumrah was visibly enraged as he watched the replay on the stadium's big screen as it demonstrated what we all saw watching live: had the decision been reviewed, Duckett would have been out as, without the aid of his pads, Bumrah's delivery would've crashed into his leg stump.

Mere minutes later the fast bowler had his revenge as the England batsman had a rather ugly swipe at a delivery he should have defended and instead, and in yet another of those pleasing moments and images only cricket can provide, Bumrah ripped Duckett's off stump clean out of the ground, sending it cartwheeling through the air behind and, in a pleasure I'll never tire of, leaving his middle and leg stumps perfectly untouched and one solitary bail still attached. Bumrah roared his approval and mere minutes later once more, he trapped the most vital England wicket of all, Joe Root, this time rightly given out LBW and even a referral to the TV umpire couldn't save the Yorkshireman.

117–3 became 140–4 with the departure of fellow Yorkshireman Jonny Bairstow for just 10 and soon after, captain Ben Stokes returned to the pavilion aghast at being clean bowled by Ravi Ashwin and with his team now deep in the mire on 163–5, they still trailed a now resurgent India by 27 runs on 1st innings and the end was seemingly nigh.

With chaos unfolding all around him, Ollie Pope had quietly and comfortably reached his 50 from just 54 balls received and now joined by Ben Foakes, they reached the Tea Break with their wickets intact, Pope 68 not out and their team still trailing by 18 runs.

Act Three: *Pope the century maker*

Following this morning's defiance and this afternoon's mini-collapse I feared a quick ending to the Test Match in the day's final session and thankfully, my fears were misplaced. Although he'd lose his wicket to a *"grubber"* of a delivery from Axar Patel that simply didn't bounce, Ben Foakes batted magnificently, taking his pre Tea total of 2 runs to a final 34 in a century partnership with Ollie Pope that frustratingly ended just 12 runs later. Rehan Ahmed then filled in and belied his tender 19 years brilliantly to end the day 16 not out but suffice to say, the honours and plaudits today fall to the man from Chelsea, Ollie Pope.

The 26 year old England vice-captain plundered 17 boundary 4's as he took his pre Tea total of 68 from 95 balls received to an eventual century from 154 balls to end the day on an arguably game saving and possibly game winning not out total of 148 from 208 balls received. He gave just one chance in an otherwise faultless display when he received a *"life"* on 110 when Axar Patel dropped a simple if high catch at the *"Backward Point"* position. From here he accumulated a further and possibly crucial 38 runs brilliantly as he continued to exhibit every shot in the book, old and new, ancient and modern, cultured and newly created: sweeping, paddle sweeping, reverse sweeping and even reverse scooping boundary 4's as an ever infuriated India team could only watch on in exasperation and utter exhaustion.

Well batted kid!

So from worrying about today and whether we had a cricketing tomorrow we do, and I couldn't be more pleased or indeed excited. Sleep will continue to evade me until later but the shrill of the alarm at 3.30am will awaken me from my slumbers to this current position:

England, against all the odds, have a lead of 126. This is by no means a winning lead, or even the prospect of one, but they also have 4 wickets in hand.

Ollie Pope is 148 not out.
Rehan Ahmed is 16 not out.

And if England can eke out another 75 runs, we'll have a hell of a finish on our hands.

India need 4 wickets and the early dismissal of Ollie Pope is vital.

They have no desire or wish to bat again in this Test Match or on this wicket.

The wicket isn't crumbling but there's spin and big variable bounce.

Chasing 175–200 runs in the 4th inning will not be easy.

But can England take 10 wickets in a day to win the Test Match?

Time will tell.

It always does.

See you in the morning!

Ben Stokes and the Patron Saint of Lost Causes

Sunday 28th January, 2024

ENGLAND 246 all out and 420 all out
INDIA 436 all out and 202 all out

England win by 28 runs

India *"won"* the opening day's play and dominated the second day's play to such an extent that their victory seemed assured by the close of play. England, with barely a positive stride forward or session victory under their belts grabbed the honours in the opening session of day 3 before being rocked back firmly into their defeated place yesterday afternoon and still trailing on first innings and with only 5 second innings wickets in hand, the spectre of defeat loomed once more on a Hyderabad horizon.

To mix my sporting metaphors, England needed snookers.

Ollie Pope ignored the chaos unfolding all around him to score a Test Match century loudly acclaimed by sages of this great game to be one of THE greatest ever by a visiting batsman in India, England had an unlikely lead, a lead they would extend by a further 104 runs this morning to turn around certain defeat into a second innings run chase for India of 231 and against all conceivable cricketing odds, England triumphed by 28 runs in a quite extraordinary Test Match for the ages and yet another reason for the longevity of this, the grandest of all games, and why I adore it so.

Quixotically, I'm not a passionate fan of the England cricket team, but hear me out. For four decades I've been obsessively in love with the game of cricket, much of which is evidenced within my first book on the grand old game *"Ashes to Ashes"*. The book became a reality through the vagaries of luck, fate, frustration and chance as well as my desire to write about a sport I excelled in as a younger man and as a spectator, I have a faintly ridiculous lifelong romantic love for. 5 days. A sporting contest that often changes with the tides of a stormy ocean. It has its own vernacular, its own pace, oddities, foibles, villains becoming heroes, today's victors becoming tomorrow's utterly defeated and dejected losers.

Some if not all of this heady sporting nonsense was evidenced here in Hyderabad.

I want England to win yes, but I **LOVE** the game of Test Match cricket far more than cheering on a singular team or indeed the country of my birth. This may seem strange to many of you but I revel in being a contrarian as much as I eagerly await the shrill of an alarm clock at 3.30am as I know that my first cup of the tea of the day will coincide with being transported to the sunshine of Mumbai or Hyderabad, Sydney or Karachi, Barbados or Brisbane. The above-named book was largely as a result of battling my mental health demons following the horrendous effects of lockdown, to allow myself to enjoy a life's sporting pleasure and of course, a reason for another of life's few remaining untainted pleasures: writing.

So I followed the England team's fortunes in the 2021/2022 Ashes debacle in Australia and their ill fated and embarrassing defeat in the West Indies soon after that led to a changing of the guard with a new coach, a new captain and, perhaps more headline grabbing, a change in the ethos to which this England team were now going to play Test Match cricket. A historic win in Pakistan soon followed before the year of 2023 started with an incredibly exciting drawn series in New Zealand before ending with one of the greatest Ashes series ever seen that England drew, could have lost, and should have won.

And if that isn't confusing enough for you it was also construed as being a *"winning draw"* as Ben Stokes' men clambered from the canvas once more to punch their Australian visitors on the nose who in fear of defeat were now thankful for the Manchester rain that fell in buckets and, winning draw or not, they retained the precious Ashes urn.

A winning draw? All part of this great game's strangely alluring lexicon.

Trust me, you'll come to love it too.

So I shouldn't have doubted Ben Stokes' England team this week or for that matter, the next 6 weeks or so of this tour of India. But visiting teams simply don't win Test Matches on Indian soil let alone a team missing Harry Brook, their front line spin bowler picking up a mid-match injury, their second spin bowler being a 19 year old leg spin bowling prodigy, their third making his Test Match debut and their singular fast bowler largely absent from bowling duties on a wicket not conducive to his sheer pace and infectious enthusiasm but perfect for the part-time bowling and *"Golden Arm"* of Joe Root, a reluctant and humble bowling hero if ever there was one.

But this Ben Stokes team did win, and a thoroughly deserved win for the ages it was too.

No session by session breakdown of events here today.

The previous three days of this Test Match were covered in this fashion and normal service will resume with the first day of the second Test Match in Visakhapatnam in five days time. Rather, let us revel in the spectacular innings of Ollie Pope who added a further 48 runs today to his stupendous total of 148 yesterday, and a match saving innings that has quickly become a match winning one. The debut of Tom Hartley who, smashed to all parts of Hyderabad in the first innings, spun his way to seven Indian wickets today, innings figures of 7–62, match figures of 9–193 and a crucial 34 runs with the bat today too in support of Ollie Pope and a combined 57 runs across the entire Test Match. 7–62 represents the fourth best bowling figures on debut in India in the entire history of this grandest of all games. 19 year old Rehan Ahmed contributed 41 runs with the bat as well as 2 first innings wickets with his prodigious leg-spin bowling. Zak Crawley and Ben Duckett set the table as well as the tone for the innings from their opening positions, Joe Root and his 5 match wickets at the cost of just 120 runs were crucial beyond words and, one minor blemish apart, Ben Foakes was outstanding with the wicket-keeping gloves whilst sharing an ultra-valuable second innings batting partnership with *"Man of the Match"*, Ollie Pope.

All of these English cricketing heroes were led by the Patron Saint of lost causes Ben Stokes, and a man who described today's victory as the ***"greatest triumph since I became captain"*** and who would dare argue with him?

To be 190 runs behind on first innings and five wickets away from a thunderously comprehensive defeat and then come back to win from being outplayed for two days is some achievement indeed. To do so in India and against a team tabling over 600 runs would be an incredible win with a first choice, fully fit, starting XI. But to do so with crucial star players absent, your talismanic number one spin bowler injured, a 19 year old in the fledgling years of a mighty cricket career ahead of him, a debutant and relying on Joe Root twirling his *"Golden Arm"* to majestic effect is indeed his greatest triumph to date and so emblematic of the revolutionary air he and Brendon McCullum breathe into this England team.

I was a fool to even doubt them.

See you in Visakhapatnam!

Jaiswal century edges India ahead on day 1 in Visakhapatnam

Friday 2nd February, 2024

INDIA 336-6

Act One: *"This kid could bat all day"*

Mid-way through the opening session of the 2nd Test Match in the coastal city of Visakhapatnam I posted the praise noted above to my oh so popular Twitter channel (@steveblackford) and so naturally come the end of the day's play with the kid in question, Yashasvi Jaiswal, having *"carried his bat"* throughout the entire day to remain overnight on a not out total of 179, I appeared to have the knowledge of a cricketing sage. Modesty prevents me from making such an outlandish statement but the kid, a 22 year old from Suriyawan in the Indian State of Uttar Pradesh, should have secured a century in the opening Test Match of this series, I had the very real pleasure of watching him plunder a debut century against an albeit weak West Indies in July last year and frankly, he looks in top form. Nerveless. Adventurous. Attacking, and with all the verve and confidence of a superstar in the making.

As always, eagerness ensures we're getting ahead of ourselves and so returning to the beginning of the day, as the television images from the other side of the world depicted the Bay of Bengal gently lapping ashore the rocky beaches of Visakhapatnam and I yearned for the nearby beaches of my youth, the 3.30am alarm clock was greeted with the news that Indian captain Rohit Sharma had won the toss and immediately announced he wished to bat first. Watching the hypnotic waves in my half awake/half asleep state, I marvelled at the perfectly circular ACA–VDCA Cricket Stadium and an ever growing crowd inside a *"high scoring venue"* and settled in with my first cup of tea of the morning, and an opening session of play that would see the home team rattling up over a hundred runs and the kid from Suriyawan not out at the Lunch Break with over 50 runs to his name.

Reaching 103–2 at Lunch it had been India's morning but this was more than a little unkind to an England team who had bowled well despite conceding over a hundred runs and had constantly pressed for further wickets whilst bowling tightly and in complimentary partnerships. Joe Root once again opened the bowling and today he accompanied the oldest swinger in town, 41 year old James *"Jimmy"* Anderson. The ageless Anderson was magnificent as always and fully deserving of more than his one wicket, that of Shubman Gill who tickled a thin edge through to wicket-keeper Ben Foakes after scoring 34 unconvincing runs.

Anderson barely leaked a run all morning, a pattern he'd brilliantly continue throughout the day.

After reaching the mid-session break for drinks on 40–0, as is so familiar to fans of this great game a wicket soon follows after the resumption of play and today it was Indian captain Rohit Sharma. It rather boggles the mind when you consider that two Test Matches into this series India have scored well in excess of 900 total runs and their talismanic free scoring leader has barely registered in the runs column. That dearth in runs continued this morning as in just the second over following the break in play, Sharma played a lazy and loose flick into the grateful hands of Ollie Pope at Leg Slip and Shoaib Bashir, forced to miss the opening Test Match due to the authoritarian bureaucracy of needing a visa to enter the country, had his first *"scalp"* and wicket on his full debut. The 20 year old from Chertsey near London would have a debut to remember as well as the forever memory of snagging the master batsman Rohit Sharma as his first ever Test Match wicket.

103–2 at Lunch signalled it was India's morning, and Yashasvi Jaiswal was just getting started.

Act Two: *Something old. Something new*

The afternoon session continued in the same vein as the morning and a pattern was set too for the day's final session later with the hosts scoring in excess of a hundred runs in each session as their visitors toiled gamely away in resistance. 122 total runs were scored in this session for the loss of only 1 wicket, that of Shreyas Iyer for 27 and after he'd finally lost his personal battle with England spin bowler, Tom Hartley. Iyer continually moved across his crease as Hartley was in his bowling stride, a habit transferred from the shorter form of the game with the batsman intimating that he's *"making room"* for an expansive shot to a lesser defended side of the field. Hartley was clearly annoyed, stopping several times mid-action to commence his routine all over again, but secured the last laugh on his opponent when Iyer under-edged a sharp catch into the wicket-keeping gloves of Ben Foakes.

Shreyas Iyer and Yashasvi Jaiswal had added 76 runs since the Lunch Break, taking their team total to 179–3 at the fall of Iyer's wicket but from hereon in, Jaiswal held centre stage. He gave just one half-chance for his wicket when on 73 and a chance that barely shouldn't register as an extra *"life"* as his flashing drive saw the ball fly through the out-stretched fingertips of Joe Root at 1st Slip.

It was hardly even a half-chance but noted here as aside from this the young batsman never looked in trouble or likely to lose his wicket as he galloped to his century from 151 balls received, the last of which from Tom Hartley he dismissively smashed into a baying crowd for a boundary 6, before reaching the Tea Break unbeaten and not out on 125 from 185 balls received.

Partnered now by debutant Rajat Patidar, the 30 year old was equally assured and nerveless as he rested at the break on 25 runs from 47 balls received and their team total an extremely healthy 225–3 after undoubtedly *"winning"* the first two sessions of the day.

Act Three: *Child's Play*

Finishing the day on 336–6, simple mathematics dictate that India scored another century of runs in the session (111) but for the first time today lost more than 2 wickets in the process. England deserved their successes as they toiled and *"plugged away"* all day long and whilst James Anderson didn't add to his haul of wickets he was magnificent once more as he barely gave away any runs and celebrated the wickets his tight bowling aided and abetted.

Leg spin bowler Rehan Ahmed snagged Rajat Patidar after he added just 7 further runs to his pre-Tea total of 25 before under-edging a wickedly spinning delivery back onto his stumps and then safely pouched a catch to dismiss the dangerous Axar Patel off the bowling of Shoaib Bashir before the debutant returned the favour and safely caught Srikar Bharat off the bowling of Ahmed when the wicket-keeper batsman had reached 17.

Once again this continued with the pattern of the day as a whole with each and every Indian batsman reaching double figures and each assisting in significant batting partnerships with Yashasvi Jaiswal, the man of the cricketing hour. Rohit Sharma partnered for 40 runs, Shubman Gill 49, Shreyas Iyer 90, Rajat Patidar 70, Axar Patel 52 and Srikar Bharat the lowest at just 29, but each and every partnership ensured their team scored well over 300 runs in the day and Yashasvi Jaiswal, an astonishing 179 of them. The kid with the flashing blade scored over half of his team's total runs today, half of the team's total boundary 4's and 5 of the team's total of 6 boundary 6's. Finishing the day on 179 not out from 257 balls received, he duly received a rapturous ovation from the Visakhapatnam crowd as well as his teammates waiting to receive him in the Pavilion after a quite incredible, and quite possibly match winning innings.

The consensus after today's play, whether it be television, radio or podcast, was that England had *"won"* the day by virtue of restricting India to just 336 runs on a wicket full of runs and snagging 6 wickets in the process. Being the arch contrarian I vehemently disagree on the basis that India have a not out batsman on 179, a batting *"tail"* full of runs and already 336 in the score books. Any team with a batsman returning just 21 runs short of a double century, 4 wickets in hand and over 330+ runs on the scoreboard must be in front after the opening day of a Test Match, but I've been wrong before.

I just choose not to publicise such failures!

But India are in front after day 1 and England need to dismiss Jaiswal early tomorrow and mop up the tail, lest they be 450+ runs adrift on 1st innings and the *"scoreboard pressure"* this brings.

Crucial first hour and opening session tomorrow.

"Boom Boom Bumrah!"

Saturday 3rd February, 2024

INDIA 396 all out and 28–0 *(leading by 171 runs)*
ENGLAND 253 all out

Oh the joys and delights, the vagaries and quintessential beauty that is the grandest of all games, Test Match cricket!

341 total runs scored in the day.

An astonishing 14 wickets tumbling.

India in the ascendancy yet falling way short of a mammoth score.

England blazing a trail until blown away as the game turned once more.

India have an almost unbeatable lead.

England are snookered behind the 8 ball needing another miracle.

Boy do I love this game!

Act One: *England win the session as Anderson rolls back the years*

Commencing the day on 336–6, India would surely have been targeting at least an extra 120 runs whilst the visiting England team desperate for the early fall of wickets and the end of their hosts 1st innings and whilst the opening 30 minutes of play was rather a stalemate, eventually England *"won"* the session, conceding just 60 further runs as they wrapped up the Indian innings for an all out total of 396.

Taking the new ball at the start of play as *"Jerusalem"* by England's visiting *"Barmy Army"* battled to be heard above the din of the air horns that would continue throughout the day, James Anderson belied his 41 years once more in an extraordinary spell of tight swing bowling that eventually snagged the outside edge of Ravi Ashwin's bat and into the gleeful gloved hands of wicket-keeper Ben Foakes. A thoroughly deserved wicket it was too, Anderson's 692nd in a record breaking Test Match cricket career and soon after, and after almost taking his wicket when on 183, Anderson would also secure the wicket of yesterday's centurion, and today's double centurion, Yashasvi Jaiswal. 19 years his junior, Jaiswal would eventually become Anderson's 693rd all-time wicket when chasing for quick runs at the end of the India innings and after the 22 year old had notched his *"double ton"*, falling for a remarkable 209 from 290 balls received.

India would add just a further 13 runs for their remaining 2 wickets as Jasprit Bumrah *"a wicket waiting to happen"* according to the sarcasm dripping through my match notes and Mukesh Kumar fell to Rehan Ahmed and Shoaib Bashir respectfully, ensuring these 2 spin bowlers and James Anderson each bagged 3 wickets and, more importantly, the hosts had arguably fallen at least 50 runs short of a targeted all out score this morning.

Batting for that cliche laden, and always ever so pleasing for an old school cricket fan such as myself, *"tricky 20 minutes"* before the end of a session, England openers Zak Crawley (15 not out) and Ben Duckett (17 not out) coasted through this shortened period to rest at the Lunch Break with their team 32–0.

It was a quite perfect morning for England in every respect: Anderson was impeccable and is now just 7 wickets away from 700 Test Match scalps. Rehan Ahmed and Shoaib Bashir (19 and 20 years of age respectively) each grabbed 3 wickets and the team as a whole had restricted their Indian hosts to below 400 on 1st innings.

The perfect morning became a sublime afternoon.

Then Jasprit Bumrah decided he wanted to come out and play!

Act Two: *"Boom Boom Bumrah!"*

From 32–0 at the Lunch Break, Zak Crawley and Ben Duckett added yet another 50 run opening partnership to their joint cricketing CV's and were calmness personified until the demise of Duckett for 21 to a beautifully spinning delivery from Kuldeep Yadav. Ollie Pope soon joined a dominant Crawley who after receiving a *"life"* when on 18 and dropped by a flying Shubman Gill at a close-in *"Mid-Wicket"* position, then rattled up a run-a-ball half century and with Pope now settling in after an unsteady start to his innings, England galloped along to 114–1 before, well, your favourite cricket correspondent fell asleep!

Oh come on!

It was *"silly o'clock"* in the morning, dawn was beginning to break with a spectacular red and purple background to the early morning clouds and Zak Crawley was looking imperious.

What could possibly go wrong?

I awoke half an hour or so later with disbelieving eyes to a picture of utter cricketing mayhem and the roars once more of Indian fast bowler, Jasprit Bumrah.

In my absence, not only had the 30 year old from Ahmedabad grabbed the vital wicket of an angry and disconsolate Joe Root for a lowly 5 runs, he'd now, spectacularly, *"castled"* Ollie Pope for 23 and in the process, smashed his middle and leg stumps clean out of the ground. This was the image I awoke to from my brief slumber, 2 of Pope's 3 stumps ripped from the ground and the constant replaying of Bumrah's incredible delivery, a fast in-swinging *"yorker"* that started way outside of Pope's off stump before spearing in like a guided missile into his middle and leg stumps. Sheer perfection. Unplayable. A *"Jaffa"* in the dictionary of this great game and what's more, no batsman in the world could have defended it. Quite beautiful. Bumrah, so ordinary this morning that Zak Crawley had pummelled him for 4 boundary 4's in just 1 over, had returned with a vengeance with the ridiculous figures of 4 overs 2 wickets for just 3 runs and if this wasn't enough, he'd improve on this further later in the day.

Sadly for England this wasn't all.

Zak Crawley, a batsman I have long championed and adore watching bat, perished for a run-a-ball 76 to the bowling of Axar Patel and being hyper critical, it was a reckless and unnecessary shot and rather than the BIG century and anchor to the innings England needed, they folded from 114–1 to 155–4 in an hour's play leading to the Tea Break and soon after, Bumrah would be back for more!

Act Three: *"Boom Boom Bumrah" (Part Two)*

All hopes now rested on Jonny Bairstow (24 not out) and captain Ben Stokes (5 not out) as England resumed after the Tea Break still a distant 241 runs adrift on 1st innings. My hopes of a huge Bairstow century disappeared immediately after the break as Bumrah claimed his third wicket of the innings and following minimal resistance from Rehan Ahmed and Ben Foakes who both fell to Kuldeep Yadav, the fast bowler then cleaned up the remainder of the England innings in yet another incredible spell of bowling that yielded figures of 6 overs 4 wickets for 14 runs and an overall innings total of 6 wickets at the cost of just 45 runs. Tom Hartley bashed a spirited 21 runs, James Anderson 6, but an image to rank with that of Ollie Pope and his shattered *"castle"* is reserved for England skipper Ben Stokes who, after bludgeoning a quick fire 47 runs from 54 balls received lost his particular castle to a delivery from Bumrah that didn't bounce and, to his utter astonishment, dribbled under his bat and into his off stump. Stokes dropped his bat on the wicket in despair and shook his head repeatedly as he trudged back to the Pavilion. Bumrah meanwhile roared in celebration at yet another wicket, and England were crawling to an all out total of just 253 to trail by a whopping 143 runs on 1st innings.

The cricket fan in me had yet another of those oh so pleasing *"tricky"* 20 minutes of no win/no lose cricket at the end of the day, but with England desperate for wickets and India keen on keeping all 10 within the Pavilion, the hosts prevailed, ending the day 28–0 and with an almost unbeatable lead after day 2 of 171 runs.

It was India's day. They've arguably *"won"* 5 of the 6 sessions hence far and commence tomorrow morning with an imposing lead, their captain Rohit Sharma 13 not out and double centurion from the 1st innings Yashasvi Jaiswal 15 not out. Tomorrow will also arguably be the best day for batting on a wicket that shows the variable bounce that accounted for Stokes and will only get lower and slower the longer the Test Match runs.

England meanwhile are in deep, deep trouble. 171 runs behind and all 10 Indian wickets still standing, they need a Herculean bowling performance from someone tomorrow to aid James Anderson in dismissing the entire India team before the lead stretches beyond 300 as it will be curtains if the lead passes 350 and next to zero fabric left if they're chasing 400+.

The history of this great game dictates this so.

They were in a huge hole after day 2 in Hyderabad but this is different. I wrote them off pre-tour and after a poor beginning in the first Test Match so I'd warmly welcome being proved wrong yet again. I foresee India piling on the misery tomorrow and the series square at 1–1 by the middle of day 4.

Hope springs eternal.

Or has it sprung a leak into the Bay of Bengal?

See you in the morning.

Shubman Gill bats England into an impossible mission

Sunday 4th February, 2024

INDIA 396 all out and 255 all out
ENGLAND 253 all out and 67–1 *(332 runs to win)*

Act One: *England's morning but India surge ahead*

Commencing day 3 on 28–0 and holding a healthy lead of 171 runs, India made the worst possible start and England, and their talismanic veteran fast bowler James Anderson, the exact opposite.

Needing quick wickets and inroads into the Indian batting order, Anderson knocked over Rohit Sharma's off stump without the Indian skipper adding to his overnight total of 13 and mere minutes later, snagged the outside edge of Yashavsi Jaiswal's bat and into the grasping hands of Joe Root at 1st Slip.

The Indian openers had added just 2 runs to their overnight total and at 30–2, England had made the perfect start to the day and Anderson had his 694th and 695th all time Test Match wickets to stand just 5 away from an incredible career milestone and just 14 more away from eclipsing the late and very great Shane Warne as the second highest wicket taker in the entire history of this, the grandest of all games. Suffice to say Anderson was magnificent as usual and unlucky not to snag a third wicket of the morning before relinquishing control of the ball to his junior spinning partners in Shoaib Bashir, Rehan Ahmed and Tom Hartley and whilst I'm sure captain Ben Stokes would've loved to continue bowling Anderson all morning long, this was as impracticable as was the frustration that his fourth part-time spinning option Joe Root had to leave the field with an injured finger and so already behind the game and desperate for further quick Indian wickets, Stokes had to turn to three spin bowlers barely out of their teens and look for a dash of luck that would long evade his energetic team. Today's man of the day Shubman Gill would be the recipient of that dash of luck as he survived two incredibly close LBW (Leg Before Wicket) appeals and referrals to the TV Umpire, one of which was only referred on advice from partner Shreyas Iyer, but inch by inch and run by run the two Indian batsmen reached the mid-session Drinks Breaks unbeaten and a blossoming partnership with Gill tabling 27 and Iyer 18.

Where Gill was counting his cricketing lives as well as his blessings, Iyer was unrushed and untroubled until bogged down and unable to score past 29, he tried to hit Tom Hartley straight for a boundary 6 and instead screwed a sky high catch that saw England captain Ben Stokes scampering backwards and sideways before taking, and holding onto, a remarkable tumbling catch.

Another great catch soon followed, albeit altogether different, as wicket-keeper Ben Foakes took a sharp chance behind the stumps from the inside edge of Rajat Patidar's bat, the 30 year old had failed with the bat once more by only scoring 9, Rehan Ahmed had a deserved wicket, and India were now 122–4 with a total lead of 265 runs.

8 runs later, India reached the Lunch Break without any further loss of wickets and especially so Shubman Gill who'd reached his half century from just 60 balls received and rested at the break 60 not out from 78 balls.

It was undoubtedly England's morning but India had still racked up a further 102 runs in the session to stretch their overall lead to 273 runs.

Act Two: *Gill the Centurion*

By the mid-session break for drinks this Test Match appeared all but over as a contest. In the hour's play since the resumption after Lunch, Shubman Gill had brilliantly smashed his way from 60 to 97 not out and all whilst being ably assisted by Axar Patel who continues to defy his critics on the TV commentary team by staking his place to bat at number 6 in this India team with a carefree 33 not out. The pair had added 76 runs in the hour's play to stretch the overall lead to an imposing 349 but yet again the official break in play saw a change in luck on the resumption of play on the other side.

Gill would reach his century, and deservedly so, from just 132 balls received and all whilst scoring 11 boundary 4's and 2 boundary clearing 6's on his flamboyant way. But he would only add a further 4 runs to his milestone before trying to reverse sweep Shoaib Bashir and in the process, gloving a looping catch into the grateful and similar gloved hands of wicket-keeper Ben Foakes. Referred to the TV Umpire, the gloved catch was as obvious as was the dismissal of his partner Axar Patel just 9 runs later for a well played 45. He too would refer his dismissal to the TV Umpire, and a delivery from Tom Hartley that scuttled along the wicket thus demonstrating the growing variable bounce that is slowly becoming more apparent and an ever present danger to every batsmen from hereon in this match.

After their swashbuckling run accumulation in the first hour of this session, India would only add a further 29 runs in the second as they edged their way to an innings score of 227–6 at the Tea Break and a total lead at this stage, and a near unbeatable one it has to be noted, of 370 runs.

Act Three: *England begin their impossible mission*

Today's third and final session was a mixture of the bizarre and the brazen, the old and the new of Test Match cricket, and a revolutionary England team chasing the impossible once more.

India began the session tentatively, barely scoring and immediately losing the wickets of Srikar Bharat and Kuldeep Yadav and had Zak Crawley held onto a rudimentary catch at 1st Slip from the bat of Ravi Ashwin, England could have cleaned up the Indian innings in a matter of minutes. But Crawley dropped Ashwin when on just 4 and nearly an hour later, an hour of strangely bizarre old school cricket as Ashwin tried to *"farm"* the strike and protect the final wickets of Jasprit Bumrah and Mukesh Kumar, he added 25 further runs before both he and Bumrah departed in quick fashion to end India's 2nd innings on 255 and a thumping lead of 398.

Needing a near-on and history suggesting impossible 399 runs to win, England naturally commenced their run chase in customary and brazen fashion as both Zak Crawley and Ben Duckett dismissively dispatched Mukesh Kumar repeatedly to the boundary on their way to a second 50 run opening partnership of the match. The only fly in the England ointment came almost immediately and the dismissal of Ben Duckett for a run-a-ball 28 and a brilliant running and diving catch from wicket-keeper Srikar Bharat from the bowling of Ravi Ashwin. Rather than sending in regular number 3 Ollie Pope for the handful of deliveries left in the day's play, England sent in *"Night Watchman"* Rehan Ahmed, who promptly crashed 2 boundary 4's, rotated the strike with Zak Crawley and was anything but the traditional block and defence expected of a Night Watchman. This England team, under those revolutionary mavericks of Ben Stokes and Brendon McCullum are not very keen on the staid and traditional!

So chasing 399 to win, England end day 3 on 67–1 needing a further 332 runs for victory with 9 wickets remaining. Here are some cricketing hors d'oeuvres ahead of your 3.30am alarm call in the morning:

If successful, this will be the 5th highest 2nd innings run chase in the entire history of Test Match cricket, an almost doubling of England's highest ever successful run chase in India set back in a long ago 1972 and 120 more runs than record holders the West Indies who hold the highest visiting run chase in India with 276.

History, past or present, traditional or revolutionary, is against England.

Will Zak Crawley turn his 29 not out into a big, match winning century?

Has Ollie Pope another match winning century in his locker?

Will Joe Root bat?

Will it come down to skipper Ben Stokes to guide his team over the line?

Or will Jasprit Bumrah blow the visitors away and restore cricketing order or perhaps Ravi Ashwin, Kuldeep Yadav and Axar Patel will spin the hosts to a comfortable win?

Despite avidly chronicling the Stokes/McCullum revolution I can't help but write them off as I did yesterday, even in spite of watching their young team rack up 500 runs in a day in Pakistan on their way to a 3–0 Test triumph, outplaying New Zealand on their own down under turf at the start of 2023 and coming as close as can be to wresting the Ashes urn away from the grasp of Australia this Summer.

The alarm is set for 3.30am and I'm writing them off again as the history of this great game resists flights of sporting fancy such as this.

But here's to James Anderson blocking at one end as his captain Ben Stokes rattles the winning runs tomorrow and the revolutionaries make yet more eye watering cricketing history.

History prevails as India level the series

Monday 5th February, 2024

INDIA 396 all out and 255 all out
ENGLAND 253 all out and 292 all out

India win by 106 runs

The alarm clock shrilled its now regular tune at 3.30am but I was already awake and enjoying my first cup of tea ahead of a long night of the soul as well as watching the grandest of all games.

I was up before the alarm for a variety of reasons, sporting and otherwise, a mix of excitement and expectation ahead of England chasing the impossible once more for sure, but sleep was always going to evade my troubled mind once I set eyes upon an old friend, and dreams flooded my cricketing brain for a love that will forever remain unrequited.

It's almost a year to the day since I celebrated being 51 not out in this strange game we call life by watching England defeat New Zealand at the Bay Oval in beautiful Mount Maunganui.

I may not have been there physically but it was easy to be in this little piece of sporting paradise in spirit, this tiny sporting venue with its grassed banks ringing the playing field waiting for wherever you decide to pitch your deckchair for the day and a day of cricket in the sunshine of New Zealand. Whilst I celebrated my birthday by watching this Test Match through the night aided and abetted as always by copious amounts of freshly brewed tea, I couldn't help but fall in love with the pleasing prospect of being there, entering the ground and choosing my *"spec"* for the day. Perhaps forego the rigid conformity of a deckchair and just sit upon the grass bank and maybe even slowly move, hour by hour or session by session, to different parts of this delightful cricket venue.

So with sleep evading me I happened upon the 2nd day of the Test Match between an incredibly strong and familiar New Zealand starting XI piling up the runs against an unrecognisable looking South Africa team with six debutants, a new captain, and what seems like a long, arduous and evolutionary cricketing journey ahead of them and then, that arrow of sporting love hit me. I was back in Mount Maunganui.

Nearly a year older. No more the wiser. Still infatuated with watching Test Match cricket through the dead of a winter's night, and still dreaming those same dreams.

It will forever be an unrequited love (unless of course you wish to whisk me to the other side of the world and then I'll be at Heathrow Airport quicker than you can say *"Air New Zealand"*) with last year's series between England and New Zealand forming the fifth and final part of my first book on cricket *"Ashes to Ashes"* and with the circular nature of this indeed strange game we call life I'll be returning to Mount Maunganui this evening, pitching my metaphorical deckchair on the grass banks before in just a few days time, celebrating being 52 not out in the game of life by watching not one, not even two, but three games of Test Match cricket on my birthday. India, Australia and New Zealand. The later trips in the evening down under will cross each other on our earthly timeline but one can't quibble with watching cricket on one's birthday for it is a rare treat indeed.

Anyway, enough of such self regarding nonsense.

History prevailed.

England chased the impossible, came up 106 runs short and India thoroughly deserved a win their match dominance should have guaranteed. It was tight, and had England's two most experienced players not inflicted their own cricketing wounds, they may even have re-written history once more.

Alas.

Rather than a session by session breakdown of the day's play as is my norm, I like to pen my thoughts on the final day's play in a different manner and so here's a UK timeline of how day 4 in Visakhapatnam unfolded with England, needing 399 to win and the fifth all time highest 4th innings run chase in the entire history of this great game starting today on 67–1, needing a further 332 runs for a spectacular victory:

4.32am Ahmed *lbw bowled* Patel 23

Last evening's *"Night Watchman"* Rehan Ahmed continued in the same vein this morning with attacking shots aplenty and clearly a *"licence"* to do so from his revolutionary leaders in captain Ben Stokes and coach Brendon McCullum. This 19 year old ball of energy and enthusiastic confidence continues to blossom since his debut a year ago in Pakistan and added 14 runs this morning to his overnight total of 9 before being trapped LBW (Leg Before Wicket) by a quicker spinning delivery from Axar Patel. In the strangely beautiful vernacular of the great game he was *"dead"* and *"plumb"* in front of his stumps and more simply and plainly out. He knew this without referring to the TV Umpire, with subsequent replays confirming Patel's quicker ball would have hit the very middle of his middle stump. But the kid had done his job perfectly, adding 23 runs to the team's total as well as protecting the senior batsmen who would now follow on a fresh new day.

4.48am Starting this morning on 29 not out, England opener Zak Crawley, a batsman I have long championed and make no apologies for continually doing so, reached his 50 from just 83 balls received and was spearheading a serene if quick chase for the historic runs required to win this Test Match. No rash, extravagant or outrageous shots. Just technically correct batting strokes for repeated boundary 4's and a continuation that saw the 26 year old from Bromley in Kent score 76 in England's 1st innings. He was in fine *"nick"* once more and looked the batsman most likely to score the big hundred needed and *"anchor"* for the innings in the run chase. Cruelly, and very unluckily, he wouldn't reach the Lunch Break.

4.57am Pope *caught* Sharma *bowled* Ashwin **23**

England vice-captain Ollie Pope raced to a run-a-ball 23 and like partner Zak Crawley, looked in fine cricketing fettle before he flashed at a delivery from Ravi Ashwin that bounced a little more than perhaps he expected. His flailing drive snagged the outside edge of his bat, flying at Indian skipper Rohit Sharma at 1st Slip who took a quite brilliant catch. All reactionary skill, no time to think or adjust his position and a catch that either *"sticks"* or it doesn't. Unfortunately for Pope and England, it stuck, and the players adjourned for the Drinks Break with England already having added 65 runs in the first hour's play but crucially, losing 2 wickets in the process.

At 132–3, England were still a distant 267 further runs from victory.

5.08am New batsman Joe Root attacks from the off, reverse sweeping consecutive boundary 4's before surviving a cigarette paper thin appeal for LBW on review. 4 minutes later would see his definitive demise.

5.12am Root *caught* Patel *bowled* Ashwin **16**

The first of England's self-inflicted wounds and whilst this revolutionary team under the guidance of Stokes and McCullum play this way, surely the ex England captain should have stayed with Zak Crawley and simply accumulated runs as the teams headed toward the Lunch Break. Instead, Root tried a spectacular shot for a boundary 6 and simply lofted a simple sky high catch for Axar Patel to pouch and for Ravi Ashwin to celebrate his 499th Test Match wicket.

England were now 154–4 and still a further 245 runs from their impossible mission.

5.52am Crawley *lbw bowled* Yadav **73**

I noted this simple sentence in my notes: *"What a cruel game this can be"*. Crawley was majestic on his way to 73 with no risk run accumulation and playing the game in front of him.

Right on the cusp of the Lunch Break he was struck on his pads by a delivery from Kuldeep Yadav that appeared both in real time and even on the TV replay to be heading down the leg side and a waste of an Umpire review that Indian captain Rohit Sharma was incredibly reticent to call for. To the shock and amazement of not just myself but both sets of players, ex England captain Alistair Cook in a UK TV studio and of course a disconsolate Crawley, the delivery was adjudged to be hitting his leg stump, the 26 year old given out, and England still a very distant 205 further runs from a now almost impossible victory.

England simply couldn't lose another wicket before the Lunch Break.

Step forward arch nemesis, Jasprit Bumrah.

5.58am Bairstow *lbw bowled* Bumrah **26**

The Yorkshireman looked comfortable throughout his stay at the crease, scoring his 26 runs briskly and from just 36 balls received. Alas his 36th and last delivery received viciously jagged inward and into his pads and yet again on review the ball was hitting his leg stump and he had to go. Lunch was immediately taken and England were still 205 further runs from victory but rather more pertinently perhaps, India were now just 4 wickets from a thoroughly dominant and deserved victory themselves.

An orange coloured crescent moon was my only companion as I lamented in the break in play that England were so near to a brilliant morning's cricket that had seen them rattle off 127 runs in pursuit of their unlikely victory only to come up against a self-inflicted wound for sure, as well as the force of nature that is Jasprit Bumrah and Ravi Ashwin on the cusp of 500 Test Match wickets amid a personal duel with Australian spin bowler Nathan Lyon for 8th place in the all time list for most wickets in this elongated and grandest of all games. Zak Crawley was unlucky. The catch to dismiss Ollie Pope was a one in a hundred wonder effort from Rohit Sharma and Jonny Bairstow just got in the way of the runaway train that is Jasprit Bumrah. With only 4 wickets remaining England were in deep trouble and with 2 fresh batsmen starting the afternoon session.

7.21am Stokes *run out* **11**

For over 40 minutes these 2 fresh batsmen, captain Ben Stokes and wicket-keeper Ben Foakes, eased their way to a comfortable 26 run partnership before England's second and decisive self-inflicted wound spelled an almost certain defeat. An easy single seemed to be in the offing as Foakes set off and his captain ambled and jogged the first part of the run before breaking into a sprint a split second too late and after Shreyas Iyer had brilliantly hit the stumps on the full. A TV replay rang the death knell on Stokes' innings, and that of his team.

7.40am *Drinks Break:* England 245–7 *(needing 154 more runs to win)*

Now joined by Tom Hartley, Ben Foakes remained England's last recognised batsman and upon whose shoulders their fate rested. Whilst Hartley, in only his second all time Test Match resisted with the bat once more to reach the break 11 not out, Foakes was comfortably 26 not out and dreams were being dreamed once more in central England that the impossible run chase was still on. With the crescent moon now replaced by the breaking of dawn and a wintry and windy English morning, those dreams would soon be dashed.

8.01am Tom Hartley receives a *"life"* and Ravi Ashwin's 500th Test Match wicket is rescinded after the England batsman is given out caught after a spectacular catch at 1st Slip by Rohit Sharma but immediately appeals as the ball hit his arm and not his batting gloves. Hartley has batted brilliantly, if in vain, once again, and now has over a hundred runs to his name across the 2 Test Matches.

8.11am Against the odds, Ben Foakes and Tom Hartley reach a battling 50 run partnership from just 63 balls received with Foakes 31 not out and Hartley 30 not out. Hope springs eternal once more with England 270–7, needing 129 more runs for victory.

8.16am Foakes *caught and bowled* Bumrah **36**

England's nemesis returns with a brilliant slower ball that fools Foakes into a false shot and straight into the returning hands of the bowler supreme.

8.32am Bashir *caught* Bharat *bowled* Kumar **0**

The 20 year old debutant ably assists Hartley for 15 minutes before edging a simple catch through to Bharat behind the stumps and England are minutes away from defeat.

8.44am Hartley *bowled* Bumrah **36**

Hartley's stout resistance is broken by the wonderful fast bowling of Jasprit Bumrah as he rips his off stump clean out of the ground to finish with innings figures of 3 wickets for 46 runs and a Test Match total of 9 wickets for just 91 runs.

This 5 Test Match series now heads to Rajkot in ten days level at 1–1.

Afterword

Whilst Ben Stokes called the decision to give Zak Crawley out as *"wrong"* he was magnanimous in defeat, described Jasprit Bumrah as a *"genius"* and sang the praises of Tom Hartley, Rehan Ahmed and Shoaib Bashir who have played *"5 or 6 Test Matches between them"*. Indian coach Rahul Dravid singled out Yashasvi Jaiswal and Jasprit Bumrah for special praise whilst also acknowledging that his team had *"left a few runs on the board in both innings"* whilst licking his lips at a *"fantastic series"* and *"there's going to be some tough cricket played over the next three games"*.

There sure is, and with that comes a dilemma dear reader. For my birthday this year comes with the sporting delight of THREE games of Test Match cricket in India, Australia and New Zealand. So we have the choice of India and England in Rajkot, Australia ladies versus South Africa ladies in Perth or New Zealand and their male South African counterparts in Hamilton.

I'll leave it up to you where we go. I'm nice like that.

Just don't forget the birthday cake!

And a mountain of candles.

Milestones galore as India take charge on day 1 in Rajkot

Thursday 15th February, 2024

Oh the joys of Test Match cricket.

Today saw the glorious spectacle of not one, not even two but three matches of the grand old game spanning the end of one cold and dark night here in England before finally ending way past the crack of dawn, the consumption of bacon and egg sandwiches and the clock ticking towards noon of another day that will end or indeed begin if you prefer, with this joyous sporting rigmarole commencing in earnest all over again.

Oh the joys of Test Match cricket.

With the evasion of the arrows of love from cupid's bow came the first of today's encounters in a faraway New Zealand and under the bluest of skies and the whitest of fluffy clouds akin to the beginning of an episode of *"The Simpsons"* and for five hours I was transfixed with a match building to a historic climax and a possible underdog win for the ages.

Next it was to the Kiwi's noisy neighbours of Australia for the first hour in Perth of the ladies Test Match between the hosts and their South African tourists before five hours after beginning my sporting quest of the day I crossed the Indian Ocean and nearly 5,000 miles at 4am for the real cricketing feast of the day and the opening day of the 3rd Test Match between a much changed India and a much rested England.

From 10pm on a cold wintry English evening to the piercing blue sunshine of Hamilton, Perth and Rajkot 13 and a half hours later. It was quite some day in the wide world of Test Match cricket, and 3 very differing examples of this quite wonderful game.

Act One: *Can the ragtag underdogs shock the Kiwis?*

Under the cartoon skies of *"Seddon Park"* in Hamilton we find an intriguing Test Match brilliantly poised and in progress after 2 full days play and, suffice to say, I've been watching this match avidly since Monday.

Winning the toss on day 1, South Africa posted a reasonable 1st innings total of 242 before bowling their hosts all out by *"Stumps"* on day 2 for 211 and thus enjoying a somewhat unexpected lead on 1st innings of 31 runs entering today's play.

I say unexpected and, to bring everyone up to date, this South African team are an experimental team of sorts, a team in transition perhaps and with several members of their regular starting XI not travelling to play the heavy, heavy favourites New Zealand, have a brand new captain, both literally and figuratively, as well as a number of debutants including a 37 year old! New Zealand on the other hand have a rock solid starting XI and whilst not the powerhouse crowned World Test Champions in 2021, still boast the veteran skills of Kane Williamson, Tim Southee and Neil Wagner as well as bright young starlets Rachin Ravindra and Will O'Rourke.

Entering day 3 trailing by 31 runs, the hosts were safe in the knowledge that they couldn't lose this 2 Test Match series having comprehensively won the opening match in beautiful Mount Maunganui by a thumping 281 runs and by the fall of the wicket of South Africa captain Neil Brand for a well played 34, they had his team and their touring visitors 39–3 and a total run lead at this stage of just 70 runs. What was even more remarkable at this very early stage in the day's play was that the *"Proteas"* skipper had scored the vast, vast majority of his team's runs this morning with 34 from a total of 39 and a template of sorts had been set for South Africa's bright young starlet of their own, David Bedingham.

An accomplished county player with a mountain of runs to his name, I had the great pleasure of watching the 29 year old Bedingham make his debut for South Africa late last year in their one-off Test Match with India, scoring a half century on debut from 87 balls received. On this new year tour of New Zealand he scored 32 and 87 in their opening match defeat and today was their star of the show with a 3rd Test Match 50 before achieving his first ever century. As with his captain Brand, Bedingham would score the vast majority of his team's runs in every batting partnership he enjoyed throughout the innings as first he reached the Lunch Break on a run-a-ball 34 (South Africa now led by 119) before reaching his half century with the innings score 100−3, his team leading by 131 runs and both he and Brand had scored 84% of the team's total runs!

By the Tea Break, Bedingham had serenely reached 88 not out from a team total of 186−4 and shortly after this official break in play and just before I turned my attention to Perth and Rajkot, the 29 year old reached his maiden Test Match century from 127 balls received and with South Africa on a 2nd innings total of 209−5, they held an imposing lead of 240 runs.

In my absence, and far more importantly the absence of a now departed Bedingham for 110, South Africa collapsed to 235 all out, losing their final 5 wickets for just 33 runs and whereas they could and should have set their Kiwi hosts a total run chase verging on the historic, they instead still set a stiff target for victory of 267.

Whether under cartoon skies or not, only once has a total of over 200 runs been successfully chased in the 4th innings at Seddon Park and that was over two decades ago. So with history against the hosts on their own turf they made a steady start to their run chase before out of form opening batsman Devon Conway fell to the second to last delivery of the day from Dane Piedt, a returnee to the fold of South African cricket and so epitomising the reinvention and evolution of the national team.

New Zealand now return on day 4 on 40–1, needing a further 227 runs to win whilst the ragtag underdogs need a further 9 Kiwi wickets for a shock victory for the ages.

Regardless, this Test Match must finish tomorrow and it's number one on my viewing schedule come 10pm this evening.

Act Two: *The agony and ecstasy of Alyssa Healy*

Leaving the beautiful grass banks of *"Seddon Park"* and my dreams of pitching up there one day with a deckchair and a day of cricket in the New Zealand sunshine, I crossed the Tasman Sea to the furthest reaches of Australia and Perth, home of the *"WACA"* ground I remember so fondly from my first ever real time watching of cricket through the night from a long ago 1987. It was the England tour of captain Mike Gatting, the consecutive centuries of Chris Broad (father of England legend Stuart), a somewhat final hurrah for Ian Botham and England in their memory evoking pyjama blue one day cricket uniforms. I was 15, in love with a girl called Susan and fast coming off the rails following the death of my dear old Dad but we don't have time today for a descent into such melancholy for we have the agony and ecstasy of Alyssa Healy to consider and first, a cricketing appreciation of Darcie Brown. As you may imagine by now I watch more than a fair amount of Test Match cricket and recall watching and admiring the swing bowling skills of 20 year old Darcie Brown since her debut for Australia in 2021. Then just 17, she showed admirable nerve for a teenager in a team full of seasoned experienced professionals and I couldn't help but admire her upright and correct bowling style as well as the prodigious amounts of swing her fast bowling produced and her wide enthusiastic smile was a constant joy to see.

Watching live today and before departing for my final cricketing destination of the day, Darcie snagged the first 2 South African wickets to fall and at 5–2 I must also note that she also had 2 catches dropped off her bowling in just her opening 2 overs and could and really should have had 4 wickets to her name mere minutes into the day's play!

Whilst South Africa recovered from the quite dreadful start of 5–2 to reach 33 runs before losing any further wickets, they then collapsed once more from 33–3 (a common score today as you're about to discover) to 50–7 before a late innings rally was extinguished by Darcie who grabbed the final 3 wickets of the innings to finish with, in the cricketing vernacular, a *"Michelle"* or *"Michelle Pfeiffer"* or more simply a *"5 fer"* or 5 for 21. 5 wickets for the cost of just 21 runs could easily have been 6 or 7 but regardless, the visiting tourists had been, cricketing vernacular once more, *"skittled"* for an all out total of just 76.

In reply, Australia shockingly collapsed themselves to 12–3 but come the crisis, enter experienced veterans Beth Mooney and captain Alyssa Healy. Regular opening partners for the one-day and T20 international team, Mooney and Healy each passed a half century in a partnership worth 155 in just 30 overs before Mooney fell 22 runs short of a Test Match century on home turf.

Joined now by Annabel Sutherland, who would notch a quick fire half century of her own from just 78 balls received to add to the 3 South African wickets she grabbed earlier in the day, the end of day honours fell to captain Healy who, after taking 2 catches with the wicket-keeping gloves and leading her team to bowling out their visitors for a paltry 76, stood on 99 not out and with the light closing in as the day was fast approaching its end, would surely scratch 1 further run into the score book for her maiden Test Match century in Australia? Alas she presented a soft return catch to bowler Delmari Tucker and the agony was etched all over her face as well as her ex colleagues and contemporaries in the TV commentary box, and the Aussie captain trudged slowly back to the Pavilion with the sportingly soul crushing score of 99.

Tomorrow will see a new day in this Test Match and one fears it will also be its final one too. Australia stand overnight with a gargantuan lead on 1st innings of 175, Annabel Sutherland 54 not out and 5 wickets still remaining. I foresee the hosts adding at least another 100 runs on 1st innings, necessitating South Africa score at least 275+ runs to even make Australia bat again and with a certain Darcie Brown in prime form, I can't see this happening and sadly, this Test Match will be over by *"Stumps"* tomorrow evening.

Thankfully, the same cannot be said for our third and final game of the day.

Act Three: *Centuries from Sharma and Jadeja see India well ahead in Rajkot*

In his first commentary stint of the tour, ex England spin bowler Graeme Swann spoke for the cricket connoisseur in all of us mad enough to sit up through a winter's night watching England when he announced his own boyhood dreams of watching England *"on the other side of the world through the night"* and *"wrapped in a duvet"* and when the drinking of tea was mentioned he was almost speaking entirely to me or certainly for me.

Minutes later he'd exclaim *"The dream start continues for Tom Hartley"* as the young spin bowler snagged a simple wicket and India, winning the toss and choosing to bat first on a placid, easy paced wicket were tumbling and stumbling to 33–3 and threatening to collapse. James Anderson and Mark Wood were bowling brilliantly in tandem and just 40 minutes into the day's play, England, much to the consternation of India captain Rohit Sharma (the local TV coverage repeatedly fixed on his exasperation at the fall of every wicket) were firmly in the driving seat and about to *"win"* the first hour of play.

Sadly for the visiting tourists this would be the only hour or session of play in which they would gain the upper hand or have any control of the day's play whatsoever and from a precarious 33–3, captain Rohit Sharma (52 not out) and new partner Ravi Jadeja (22 not out) would steer India to 93–3 at the Lunch Break, 185–3 at the Tea Break, and both men would rest at the break on the precipice of their own individual century milestones.

Man of the day Sharma, so devoid of runs in the series hence far, would take his pre-Tea total of 97 quickly to his century post-Tea before becoming Mark Wood's third wicket of the day and falling for a brilliantly made 131 from 196 balls received. He received two extra *"lives"* when on just 27 he was dropped by Joe Root at 1st Slip before in the very next over when on 29 he overturned an umpire's decision to give him out LBW (Leg Before Wicket) from the bowling of James Anderson and with these additional cricketing lives, he notched a majestic century of extra, and very probably, costly, match changing runs.

Ravi Jadeja would be far more circumspect in his run accumulation than his captain as he inched to his half century from 97 balls received before finally, and seemingly very nervously, he secured both his Test Match century from 198 balls received and notching his 3,000th career Test Match run in the process.

But this was not all.

As Jadeja, in the cricketing vernacular for the final time, *"scratched around"* in the (sorry, one final time) *"nervous 90's"*, he barely scored as he inched his way, single run by single run, to 99 not out. This was all a far cry from new partner and debutant Sarfaraz Khan who took his long awaited debut for his country with panache and aplomb, racing to a 48 ball half century, smashing 7 boundary 4's and 1 boundary clearing 6 in the process and fulfilling all the excitable headlines written about the talented 26 year old from Mumbai.

A star was quickly born today and then, calamity struck.

With Jadeja seeking that single run to reach his individual milestone, Khan, in his eagerness to help his teammate reach his century, took off for a run that was never there and sent back by Jadeja, was stranded way out of his crease when Mark Wood swooped in and with only one stump to aim for, hit it directly, uprooting it spectacularly from the ground, England had a gift wicket out of nothing, Jadeja was still 99 not out and Khan run out for a wonderfully played if heart breaking in its ending, 62.

But day 1 belongs fairly and squarely to the hosts and with a total of 326–5 at *"Stumps"*, India have taken full advantage of a batter friendly wicket to pile on a substantial 1st innings total with a centurion still not out overnight and 5 wickets still remaining.

Tomorrow is another day and a somewhat special one for your favourite cricket correspondent as I'll be celebrating being 52 not out in this strange game we all call life and I'll be commemorating the day in an incredibly niche way by first dreaming of sitting on the grass banks surrounding *"Seddon Park"* in Hamilton, then watching the Australian ladies pile on the runs against their South African rivals in the memory evoking *"WACA"* of Perth before hoping England keep a rampant India below 400 1st innings runs in Rajkot.

3 games of Test Match cricket accompanied by oodles of tea and chocolate biscuits all whilst wrapped within a duvet to beat away the cold of an English winter's night?

Niche, but it'll do for this cricket loving madman.

Then a stroll along the riverbank in the shadow of the world's oldest iron bridge and a bag of piping hot chips with my favourite person in all the world.

Perfect.

Duckett century signals spectacular England fightback in Rajkot

Friday 16th February, 2024

One double centurion.

Two stunning individual centuries.

Three vastly different ways of reaching the *"magical three figures"*.

It was quite some day once more in the wide world of Test Match cricket and here it is, as it must be, in three sporting Acts:

Act One: *Kane Williamson — The master batsman supreme*

As I dreamed once more of attending the quaint, picturesque and tree lined oval cricket grounds of New Zealand their favourite cricketing son and national idol Kane Williamson was writing his own script once more. The story of the day was a simple one to write but New Zealand's eventual, record breaking victory of 7 wickets whilst looking overwhelmingly dominant and comfortable was far from the 7 wicket win that will forever now be etched in the sport's score book.

Commencing the day's play on an overnight 2nd innings score 40–1, New Zealand needed a further 227 runs to win and become only the second team ever in the history of the game to score 200+ runs in the 2nd innings to win at Hamilton's beautiful *"Seddon Park"*. To upset the cricketing applecart for an underdog win for the ages, South Africa needed 9 wickets. But Kane Williamson simply produced an ultra professional performance as well as a masterclass in elongated determination not to be bested or lose his wicket and on paper at least, his nation secured a comfortable looking 7 wicket victory.

But it was never easy or comfortable as South Africa captain Neil Brand (who must take immense credit for the manner in which he cajoled the ragtag team around him as well as the inventive field positions that led to the demise of both New Zealand wickets to fall today, and in an almost mirror fashion too) as well as the rotation of bowlers Tshepo Moreki and Shaun von Berg around strike bowlers Dane Paterson and Dane Piedt. Every bowler deserved a wicket, especially debutant Shaun von Berg and Dane Paterson (who's *"snorter"* to Kane Williamson mid-innings was the very dictionary definition of *"unplayable"* and a joy to re-watch on constant replay) but only the immensely impressive Dane Piedt secured wickets today, and his total of three was sadly never enough for the battling tourists.

If the *"Proteas"* are in transition and evolution as I continually posit that they are, then they have a backbone of a starting XI going forward under the stewardship of Neil Brand.

But today was all about Kane Williamson and a master innings seemed inevitable from the very first delivery of the day and I can only describe his display as masterful, pugnacious, determined and ultra, ultra professional. Led by Williamson, New Zealand scored 67 runs for the loss of Tom Latham in the first session of play and 66 runs for the loss of Rachin Ravindra in the second to leave them chasing 94 runs to win in the day's third and final session. Williamson himself scored 44 and 48 in these opening two sessions to rest at the Tea Break 92 not out from 176 balls received and after securing his 32nd Test Match century minutes after the resumption of play, I departed for my second Test Match of the day across the Tasman Sea in Australia.

In my absence, Williamson's batting partner Will Young scooted his pre Tea total of just 11 not out to an eventual 60 not out whilst Williamson added a further 33 runs to his century and a seemingly comfortable victory by 7 wickets. But South Africa may be on the rise again in the coming months and years and Test Match cricket needs a strong and vibrant South Africa for the game to continue to thrive.

Kane Williamson's 32nd Test Match century sees the 33 year old and 14 year veteran of the grand old game in 25th spot in the all time list of run scorers and just 100+ runs away from eclipsing luminaries such as AB de Villiers of South Africa, VVS Laxman of India and David Warner of Australia, and a further 350+ runs from overtaking Graham Gooch of England to become the 18th all time top run scorer in the history of Test Match cricket. Last evening was a joy to watch.

Kane Williamson — The master batsman supreme.

Act Two: *"Annabel Sutherland is made for Test Match cricket"*

Apart from a solitary hour, the ladies one-off Test Match in Perth and the third match in a series of five between India and England criss-cross each other's timeline and hence I only watched an hour's play in real time today before tuning into my main event, but the unequivocal story of the day was being played out in Perth's famed "WACA" cricket ground. After bowling South Africa all out for a tepid and paltry 76 before gallivanting to a gargantuan 1st innings total of 251–5 and an overnight lead on 1st innings of 175, Australia stretched their lead by 39 runs in the hour's play I watched live and Annabel Sutherland continued where she left off yesterday by reaching 71 not out before I turned my attention to Rajkot in India.

In my absence and now via a ten minute highlights package, the 22 year old from Melbourne reached her second all-time Test Match century (and first on her home turf of Australia) with consummate ease before running through the batting gears on her way to a stunning 150 and then, according to the sexiest voice in all cricket Mel Jones, she reached *"the most magnificent double hundred you will ever see in Test Match cricket"* with a beautifully lofted straight drive for a boundary 4. Sutherland would add a further 10 runs before finally being dismissed for an astonishing 210 from just 256 balls received, collecting 27 boundary 4's and 2 boundary clearing 6's on her merry way into the cricket record books forever more. Ably assisted by Ashleigh Gardner (65), Sophie Molineux (33) and Kim Garth (agonisingly left 49 not out), Aussie captain Alyssa Healy declared their 1st innings on a mighty 575–9 and a faintly ridiculous lead on 1st innings of 499 runs!

I posited in yesterday's journal that Australia would wrap up this Test Match victory today but I hadn't bargained for Annabel Sutherland crashing a double century or her captain Alyssa Healy wanting her team to continue batting for the vast majority of the day. But with South Africa needing to score 500 runs just to make Australia bat again and already deep in a hole at 67–3 on 2nd Innings, this Test Match is ending tomorrow, and in a historic winning fashion for the World Champion Aussies.

Act Three: *Duckett leads England fightback with spectacular century*

Turning my attention in conclusion to day 2 from Rajkot, it was a day of Test Match cricket that nearly had the cliched *"everything"*, veered wildly from one team to the other in terms of dominance, had the spectre of niggling injuries so common on a tour of this length, dropped catches from a usual exemplary England, the ultra rare penalty of 5 runs being awarded to England following Ravi Ashwin constantly running on the sacred centre of the wicket and then to top matters in an ever confusing manner, India battled brilliantly to a 1st innings runs total still 50 runs short, 50 too many for their visitors from England, who then promptly knocked off over 200 runs of their deficit on 1st innings in just under 3 hours of thrilling playing time.

Returning to the beginning of the day, England made as perfect a start as they did on day 1 by quickly removing Kuldeep Yadav (a brilliant out-swinger from James Anderson and his 696th all time Test Match victim) and yesterday's centurion Ravi Jadeja brilliantly *"caught and bowled"* by Joe Root after stifling the batsman, frustrating him by cutting off any easy runs and forcing a false shot straight into his gleeful hands. England had taken 2 quick wickets for the cost of just 5 runs to India's overnight total of 326–5 and now on 331–7, the tourists scented blood and a maximum total of 400.

Overnight, India will no doubt have been targeting 500 and so to finish on 445 all out would seem to be a happy medium yet still a frustrating runs total for both teams.

That India reached 445 all out was down to Ollie Pope and Ben Stokes dropping easy late innings catches and the nagging partnerships of Dhruv Jurel and Ravi Ashwin and tail-enders Jasprit Bumrah and Mohammed Siraj.

A wicket-keeping batsman on debut, a legendary spin bowler and two fast bowlers simply took aim at the England bowling and flailed a combined 122 runs between them and at the mid-innings changeover before the day's final afternoon session, India were well and truly in the ascendancy.

England openers Zak Crawley and Ben Duckett had to negotiate yet another of those tricky *"no-win"* 20 minutes of batting pre the Tea interval but did so without alarm and notched 31 runs in the process. Resuming for the day's final session, Crawley simply couldn't get going and would eventually fall to the bowling of Ravi Ashwin and his 500th all-time Test Match wicket that sees this future legend of the game just 17 wickets away from overtaking his Australian spin bowling contemporary Nathan Lyon and a further 2 away from surpassing West Indian great Courtenay Walsh to be the 7th highest wicket taker in the entire history of the game.

Yet it was to be Ashwin's only wicket of the session as he and his Indian teammates were caught in the whirlwind of Ben Duckett who had got started, racing to 19 not out prior to the Tea Break before scoring a faintly ridiculous 114 runs in the final session alone to end the day 133 not out.

There are no real adequate words to describe Duckett's innings post the Tea interval. I've watched Australian David Warner hit a century in a session live, as I did England's Harry Brook on the 2022 tour to Pakistan. But this was extraordinary, spectacular and defied my eyes to confirm they weren't lying to me. He raced to 50 from just 39 balls as he shared yet another half century opening partnership with Zak Crawley before repeatedly rapping boundary 4's and 6's on his way to a 88 ball hundred and 133 not out overnight from just 118 balls received.

Indian captain Rohit Sharma moved the field.

Ben Duckett simply hit the ball to a different part of the boundary.

Rinse and Repeat!

A quite incredible century in a day full of them.

The only fly in the England ointment was the late and unlucky dismissal of Ollie Pope for 39 as the vice-captain looked in prime form for yet another century, but Joe Root (in desperate need of a Test Match century) accompanies Ben Duckett in the morning with England resuming on 207–2 and 238 further runs behind India on 1st innings.

Here's the revolutionary rub:

This England team under the revolutionaries par excellence Brendon McCullum and Ben Stokes will attack from the off tomorrow and if it comes off, as so often has been the case since the tour of Pakistan in 2022, they'll not only match India's 1st innings total but exceed it by 100+ runs come the end of day 3. But someone has to make that BIG score, Duckett maybe, Root's much needed century perhaps or a masterclass from captain Stokes, but they have to bat all day tomorrow and bat big.

England's revolutionaries never take a backward step and are revolutionising this grandest of all games for a new audience and a new sporting age. But I have a devil on each shoulder watching this England team, arguably perhaps the highest of all compliments. One says they have to *"dig in"*, be solid and accumulate runs without being reckless. The other says *"fuck it!"*, attack, attack, attack, foot on the opponent's throat and really go for the jugular à la Australian World Champion teams, past and present.

It sure is a ride watching this England team, and Ben Duckett's innings today is a shining example of the revolutionary fervour running rampant through a team determined to leave their mark on the storied history of this great and wonderful game.

Revolutionaries Routed in Rajkot
Saturday 17th February, 2024

I concluded yesterday's journal giddy with excitement and by proclaiming that England needed to bat *"big"* in the sport's vernacular, bat India *"out of the game"* and bat all day.

They didn't even make it past my first pack of chocolate digestives!

England's tale of woe, with added commentary from either the television or the chocolate addled mind of your favourite cricket correspondent:

Root *"Oh Joe! Why have you played that shot now!"* **(18)**
Bairstow *"Good fucking luck playing that ball!"* **(0)**
Duckett *"Oh don't get out to a lousy long hop!"* **(153)**
Stokes *"England are in trouble now"* **(41)**
Foakes *"2 in 2 balls!"* **(13)**
Ahmed *"Another wicket for Siraj!"* **(6)**
Hartley *"Another one! He get's his revenge! Jadeja!"* **(9)**
Anderson *"Make that number 4!"* **(1)**

With England rattling up 207 runs in double quick time yesterday afternoon in response to India's 1st innings total of 445 I was indeed giddy with sporting excitement for today's play but I also hedged my bets, urged for a little caution and for someone to follow Ben Duckett's example with a big century ensuring parity on 1st innings at the very least and at the very best, a game changing lead. Ex England legendary spin bowler and entertaining TV co-commentator these days Graeme Swann described Kuldeep Yadav as bowling a *"masterclass"* and I couldn't help but reluctantly agree. Mohammed Siraj emerged from the overwhelming shadow of Jasprit Bumrah and throw in a couple of calamitous and horrendous errors, England collapsed from an overnight position of 207–2 to 319 all out and rather than rampaging their revolutionary way to a lead on 1st innings, they were all out in a session and a half of play to trail by a distant 126 runs.

Ben Duckett has more than enough credit in the bank to be forgiven for dumping a dreadful *"long hop"* straight into the hands of Shubman Gill but Joe Root danced with the revolutionary devil and chuntered all the way back to the Pavilion a dejected man and England had added just 53 runs to their overnight total.

It was as good as this morning would get.

Co-commentator Nick Knight was correct in his proclamation that England were in trouble following the departure of captain Ben Stokes for a carefree and carefully created 41, but 20 total runs and a rampaging Mohammed Siraj later, they were all out for a lowly 319 having lost their final 7 wickets for just 95 runs.

The second Act of our sporting play today contained another Indian masterclass, this time from 22 year old Yashasvi Jaiswal who was simply *"playing England at their own game"* in the words of Graeme Swann and instructed to *"take a bow"* from fellow spin bowling legend of yesteryear Ravi Shastri when he reached a quite spectacular century from just 122 balls received. Jaiswal accelerated from his rather sedate and circumspect 19 not out at the Tea Break by repeatedly crashing Tom Hartley to the boundary, reaching his half century with a ginormous drive for a boundary 6 on his way to a 42 ball second half century before having to *"retire hurt"* due to a back spasm.

This kid is so good he even managed to finagle a *"retired hurt"*, so long in retirement in the modern game and a quaint anomaly so befitting the grand old game, back today, and back into today's headlines.

Well batted kid.

But in those same Indian headlines I dare suggest that Shubman Gill will also be featuring heavily as he kept his partner company throughout the afternoon and long into the evening in a 150+ run partnership and remains not out at *"Stumps"* on 65, his team enjoying a thumping lead of 322 runs with 8 wickets remaining, and the destiny of the game seemingly and completely in their hands. Indian captain Rohit Sharma will have the West Indies all-time 4th innings run chase of 418 in May 2003 as a first port of call and then will surely seek a lead of 500 before unleashing his bowlers late tomorrow afternoon. From experience, this is pretty customary fare for a team in such a dominant position. But Sharma will have that nagging doubt that 500 runs, even though the entirety of Test Match cricket suggests otherwise, is still achievable from these revolutionary Englishmen whose mantra is always *"we'll chase down anything"*.

From a position of dominance England have been thoroughly outplayed today and to a point that Test Match cricket history suggests they simply cannot now win this Test Match. They will surely now be set a target far in excess than has ever been scored to win batting last in the 4th innings of a Test Match since records began.

The revolutionaries have been routed.

For today.

Our third and final Act returns us all once more across the Tasman Sea to Perth in Australia for the hosts' wholly expected and overwhelmingly dominant victory by an innings and 284 runs over a plucky if over-matched South Africa. Despite a debut Test Match half century from Delmari Tucker and an elegant maiden Test Match half century from Chloe Tryon, and within an innings containing 10 boundary 4's and each one a true gem of a *"correct"* cricket shot through the covers, Alyssa Healy's World Champion Australian ladies team cruised to a dominant win.

Today's game sealing wickets were shared among Darcie Brown, Ellyse Perry, Ashleigh Gardner and Alana King together with *"Player of the Match"* Annabel Sutherland who snagged 2 wickets today to go with the three scalped in the 1st innings, as well as the small matter of her double century yesterday with the bat!

The spectre of *"one-off"* Test Matches continues to haunt the ladies game and a game currently holding a stratospheric popularity as so well evidenced during last year's sold out Ashes series between Australia and England.

I have completed a rudimentary search of the fixture list for every premier cricket playing nation and whilst England have a heavy summer workload as regards one-day cricket and South Africa host Sri Lanka for 6 one-day internationals between April and May of this year, Australia have zero upcoming fixtures (although they have played almost constantly since the Ashes last summer) but the recurring factor is the lack of any ladies Test Match cricket scheduled in the calendar and I'd hazard a guess we now have to wait until the next Ashes series for our next 5 day game Test and it'll probably be a *"one-off"* Test too.

The longer form of Test Match cricket has never been in such rude health. Let's have some more of it please, and in a *"series"* format rather than repeated *"one-offs"* and all games to take place, as with Perth and its storied history *"WACA"* ground this week, in Grade A Test Match venues around the world.

Hardly a revolutionary idea is it?

India rampage to thunderous victory in Rajkot

Sunday 18th February, 2024

I have officially aged another calendar year in this absurdist game we all call life during this Rajkot Test Match and I dare say, though he would be loathe to admit it to anyone, Ben Stokes may have aged a year or three too during the past four days in the Indian sunshine. At 33–3 his English revolutionaries had their hosts and cricketing counterparts on the ropes early on day 1 and had Joe Root taken a fairly rudimentary slip catch to dismiss Indian captain Rohit Sharma with the score on 47–3, who knows where, and in which direction, this sporting dance may have taken us. Instead, Sharma batted his way back into form with a match changing century and yet he won't have been anywhere near consideration for the *"Man of the Match"* award as even Yashasvi Jaiwal's incredible double century (his second such feat in the opening three matches of this series) wasn't enough to eclipse Ravi Jadeja and his match changing 1st innings century, combined match bowling figures of 7 wickets for 95 runs and his magical spell of bowling today as his 5 wickets for just 41 runs ripped the heart and soul from the England batting order once more.

Aside from the opening hour of play on day 1 and Ben Duckett's fantastical century in the final session of day 2, England haven't so much had their backs to the wall but were nailed firmly to it by a dominant and rampant India team now taking a 2–1 series lead with them to Ranchi in five days time. Set 557 to win and over 100 runs in excess of the 418 scored by record holders the West Indies in 2003 and the highest ever 4th innings run chase for victory in the entire near two centuries of history wrapped around this grandest of all games, fanciful dreams were had of England rampaging their way to the greatest Test Match win of all time. Instead they folded like a pack of cards eerily reminiscent of so many England batting collapses of the past and an infamous December morning in Melbourne in 2021 when Scott Boland had the time of his life as the English *"Poms"* were ground into the Australian dust in 81 painful minutes.

Another year older should see me another year to the wise but as I posited at the end of day 2, I was a believer and with a dominant day 3 England could bat India completely out of the game, setting up the historic win their opponents are now taking with them to Ranchi. But England collapsed and rather than parity on 1st innings let alone a huge lead, they found themselves this morning staring down the barrel of a run deficit of 322 before a severely increased and faintly ridiculous 557 runs to chase for an absurd if history shattering win.

Yet I still believed as I've been a member of the Stokes/McCullum revolutionary cult since the beginning and hoped I'd have to disbelieve my own lying eyes one more time. Watching cricket through the night, night after cold English night with only an inexhaustible supply of tea and biscuits can do that to a man, even a man and fanatic of this incredible game in his 52nd year on Planet Starbucks.

There shall be no recriminations or questioning of their *"Bazball"* style for today's humbling and dare I say humiliating defeat by a thumping and quite extraordinary 434 runs and second heaviest Test Match defeat of all time. They were simply outplayed by a thoroughly dominant India who demonstrated exactly why in just today's play alone, scoring an additional 235 runs to stretch their lead to 557 before in just over 2 hours of play, bowling England all out for just 122. Mark Wood top scored with 33 after some lusty late innings blows to the boundary but England consistently collapsed to 28–4, 50–7 and 91–9 before his late intervention. A calamitous run out of Ben Duckett started the rot before Jasprit Bumrah removed his opening partner Zak Crawley and from 18–2 onward, the spinning trio of Ravi Jadeja, Ravi Ashwin and Kuldeep Yadav went to work, snagged combined figures of 8 wickets for just 79 runs between them, and were damn near unplayable at times.

There were no real rash shots or *"Bazball"* style (whatever that is) reckless attempts to attack the game. They simply weren't allowed to by a roaring and rampaging Indian team on their way to a thoroughly dominant win and an utterly dispiriting defeat inflicted upon their English revolutionaries and visitors.

A historic win for the ages for India.

A humbling for a thoroughly defeated England.

Afterword

Ben Stokes: ***"Everyone has got a perception and opinion. The people in the dressing room are the opinions that really matter to us. Sometimes things don't work out how we want them to. 2–1 down and two games left. We have a great opportunity for 3–2. We leave this game behind us and know we have to win the next two games to win the series".***

Rohit Sharma: ***"When you play Test cricket, it's not played over two days or three days. We know the importance of staying in the game for five days. They put us under pressure, we've got class in our squad when it comes to bowling. The message was to stay calm, it's easy to drift away from what you want to do. I'm proud of how we came back, and when that happens it's a delight to watch".***

Root grinds a priceless century for England on day 1 in Ranchi

Friday 23rd February, 2024

ENGLAND 302-1 *(Joe Root 106 not out)*

Retreating to bed early on Thursday evening in a middle England approaching freezing and under the fullest of moons, I awoke less than an hour later and it wasn't only due to the madness that a full moon can often bring to a troubled mind. I'd made the twin fatal mistakes of having a short afternoon nap before listening to the *"Test Match Special"* podcast, and that British, dare I say, world broadcasting institution, relayed tales live and direct from Ranchi, and a wicket that was troubling and baffling everyone. Legend has it that Ranchi is a cricket ground full of runs but this wicket drew long and protracted discussions from both teams with Ben Stokes proferring that it was *"interesting"* and presumably with an eyebrow raised skyward in sporting befuddlement. A cricketing term such as *"crazy paving"* would seem to be the picture painted, an already cracked and scarred surface with an *"interesting"* patch of worn wicket that will trouble every batsman as well as being a racing certainty that the wicket will quickly become lower and slower, and more and more difficult to bat on as the contest enters days 3 and 4.

Act One: *Akash Deep and a debut to remember*

England captain Ben Stokes won the toss and chose to bat. He announced two changes to his team from the mauling in Rajkot with Ollie Robinson and Shoaib Bashir replacing Mark Wood and Rehan Ahmed respectively. Holding a 2–1 series lead, Indian captain Rohit Sharma confirmed the resting of talismanic fast bowler Jasprit Bumrah for the final match in Dharamshala in two weeks, with 27 year old Akash Deep, his Test Match debut making replacement. England would end the opening session on 112–5 and teetering on the brink of collapse. Akash Deep had scalped 3 of the 5 wickets to fall and in an hour's cricket he'll never forget. But two deliveries defined the morning's play from Ranchi, and they arrived at an England batsman almost exactly two hours apart.

The first delivery from debutant Akash Deep lifted viciously from a standard cricketing *"length"* to rap England opener Zak Crawley high on his gloves. It was an incredible delivery in Deep's first over in Test Match cricket, leaving the 6 ft 6 batsman with a startled, hassled and high defensive shot. With the Lunch Break one delivery away and England 112–4, captain Ben Stokes would have seen the morning's play as somewhat of a triumph for this team in the testing conditions. One delivery later, a ball from the spinning fingers of Ravi Jadeja simply didn't bounce, at all, skidding along the wicket before crashing ankle height into his boot.

Stokes didn't even trouble the TV umpire and simply turned for the Pavilion, laughing, smiling and shaking his head in utter astonishment. In two hours, the Ranchi wicket had seen England's tallest player fending off a throat high missile and their captain defeated by a *"grubber"* that refused to bounce.

This Test Match is already shaping up to be a humdinger!

Despite England's solid and then accelerating start due to the imperious shot making of Zak Crawley, the session belonged to India with their debut maker Akash Deep leading the team from the field of play at Lunch. He bowled throughout the opening hour and rested at the Drinks Break with all 3 England wickets to fall to his name and it could, and so very spectacularly should, have been 4. Deep finished the first hour's play with figures of 3–20 and within the space of 15 balls accounted for the edge snagged from the bat of Ben Duckett, the LBW decision that saw Ollie Pope fall for a 2 ball *"duck"* and then the cricketing *"peach"* of a delivery that cut Zak Crawley in half before crashing into his off stump. It was a real beauty of a delivery and an exact replica of an earlier delivery to Crawley that beat him even more comprehensively before spectacularly sending his off stump cartwheeling through the air.

His *"no ball"* was unforgivable (as are **ALL** no balls) and it cost his team a further 38 runs from a reprieved Crawley, but he got his man in the end and after just an hour's play he had 3 Test Match wickets to his name.

The second hour of the day followed the above pattern with a slowly accelerating partnership developing between Yorkshire mates of many Test Matches Jonny Bairstow and Joe Root, as well as the late tumbling of wickets. Bairstow heavily outscored his county and country colleague before trying to sweep Ravi Ashwin and he was *"dead"* and *"plumb"* on live viewing let alone the TV replays and eventual referral to the TV umpire. 17 balls later, Ravi Ashwin's spin twin Ravi Jadeja bowled a ball to Ben Stokes that necessitated the England captain wearing a Hi-Viz jacket and using a shovel rather than a cricket bat, and India had *"won"* the morning session.

Act Two: *Root and Foakes steady the England ship*

At 5.28am I posted this Pink Floyd inspired balderdash to the wild, weird and occasionally wonderful world of the social media platform formerly known as Twitter:

"Every time Joe Root is at the crease I'm convinced today is the day he'll cream a century. I'm clearly a hex of some kind. Is hex the right word? Fucked if I know. It's 5.20am, I haven't slept, it's a full moon, and the lunatics are on the grass".

It seems my use of hex was correct and far more importantly, the ex England captain was finally ready to banish the curse I've unwittingly placed upon him. You see, occasional match aside when life has gotten in the way, I've watched the entirety of Joe Root's international career and, even if I say so myself, a firm supporter of his captaincy even after the dreadful showing in the 2021–2022 Ashes series with Australia (please see my previously published book *"Ashes to Ashes"* for further evidence) and for the simple fact he was England's best player and needed to steady the team through some turbulent cricketing seas. I have been proven wholly incorrect by the Ben Stokes/Brendon McCullum axis and style of play since Root resigned as captain but he's continued to pile on the runs to sit 10th in the all time list of most Test Match runs in the entire history of the game. 1,000 more runs will see Root jump to 5th and ahead of England's all-time run-maker Sir Alistair Cook and I see no reason whatsoever why the 33 year old Yorkshireman can't match 41 year old James Anderson for playing years and hence Root could go close to Sachin Tendulkar's staggering record of 15,921 Test Match runs. All of which is for a far away future.

In the here and now or at least the afternoon session today, Root batted faultlessly for the entire session and alongside wicket-keeper batsman Ben Foakes added 86 runs in the session to take the team total to 198–5 at the Tea Break.

Starting the session on 16 not out, Root scored the majority of the runs accumulated this afternoon as he first reached the Drinks Break 43 not out, his 30th Test Match 50 from 108 balls received before resting at the Tea Break undefeated on 67. Partner Foakes started the session fresh and from 0 he eased his way to 18 not out by the mid-session break before resting his bat for Tea on 28 not out.

86 runs added without the blemish of a lost wicket, England had *"won"* their first session of the day, and the hex upon Joe Root was soon to be banished.

Act Three: *Root the Centurion as England take the honours on Day 1*

Joe Root's 31st Test Match century came via a beautiful *"off-drive"* that pierced the close-in Indian fielders, from a total of 218 previous balls received and after watching partners Ben Foakes (47) and Tom Hartley (13) fall to the expensive bowling of Mohammed Siraj along the way. There wasn't any great celebration for his achievement, not a leap in the air or a guttural roar. Just a simple raising of his bat and back to the task in hand. The ex-captain entered the fray this morning with England 47–2 after losing 2 quick wickets from 3 brilliant deliveries from Indian debutant Akash Deep and, as was so often the case during his tenure as captain, he entered the field of play with his team struggling and their backs to the wall.

He left the field of play today 106 not out and will be returning in the morning with Ollie Robinson already a healthy 31 not out in an unbroken partnership of 57 and England, whisper it, ahead of the game and 302–7.

Tomorrow's first session of play is vital to this Test Match. The onus is on Root and Robinson to score the majority of the additional runs in the morning and if they can eke out another 75–100, England will have a dominant looking 1st innings total on the scoreboard. Conversely, if India can winkle out the final 3 England wickets for a handful of runs, England will still hold sway but the game will be far more evenly poised.

"Ben Stokes didn't need a bat then, more a Hi-Viz jacket and a shovel".

Stephen Blackford, listening to the early morning bird song in middle England before the sporting chaos resumes. A bacon sandwich and a strong brew is a distinct possibility.

So I posted to Twitter at 6.34am. 4 glorious hours later, Joe Root had his 31st Test Match century and had made rather a mockery of a wicket than can only get slower, lower and drastically more unpredictable as the game wears on. I'd posit more batsmen than Ben Stokes will need a shovel on this wicket come the weekend.

Game on.

Bashir tightens the screw as England dominate in Ranchi

Saturday 24th February, 2024

ENGLAND 353 all out *(leading by 134 runs)*
INDIA 219-7

Commencing day 2 on 302–7, England would stretch their overall advantage on 1st innings by a tick over 50 runs to 353 all out. By the close of play *"Stumps"* this advantage had shrivelled to 134 runs but in this grandest of all games England's theoretical *"lead"* and dominant position in a Test Match they dare not lose had in fact increased, their overnight dominance from day 1 extended, and they will now enter day 3 with the whip hand having had an almost perfect day, a day broken, as is tradition, into three cricketing acts.

Act One: *All's fair in love and (sporting) war*

England's almost perfect day first saw Ollie Robinson taking his overnight not out total of 31 through to his first ever Test Match 50 as he largely dominated the run scoring in his continuing partnership with yesterday's centurion, Joe Root.

Passing a century batting partnership, Robinson became the first of 3 wickets to fall in quick succession to the bamboozling spin of Ravi Jadeja, but the batting group as a whole had accomplished their morning mission of adding 50+ more runs to their 1st innings total. Yesterday's headliner and centurion Joe Root added 16 runs to his overnight not out total to remain unbowed, unbroken, undefeated and 122 not out. As I said, it was an almost perfect day for England. With 45 minutes to play until the Lunch Break and a Ranchi crowd growing larger and larger with every passing minute, Indian opening batsmen Rohit Sharma and Yashasvi Jaiswal strode toward the *"dried up riverbed"* of a wicket under leaden skies more fitting Old Trafford in Manchester and therefore perfect for one of its favourite ever sons.

Crowds in India grow quickly in size when their local heroes are batting and perhaps it's a culture of a wider world of watching cricket. Being ever the contrarian, I prefer watching England when they're bowling as I've watched too many batting collapses to last me a lifetime and being the ex fast bowler of my youth, I love rooting and roaring them on when they have that red cricketing *"cherry"* in their hand, or more specifically, when James Anderson does.

Burnley born but son of Manchester and Old Trafford Cricket Ground where an *"end"* is named after him, I've watched James Anderson his entire career and every season the 41 year old says he's going to continue playing Test Match cricket is a season and a reason to be cheerful. His bowling style has been honed to perfection over the years but is still poetry in motion, his Glenn McGrath machine like ability to hit that difficult *"length"* for batsmen a feat for a legend and the very reason why India captain Rohit Sharma became Anderson's 697th all-time Test Match wicket today. A perfect delivery from Anderson that kissed the surface before jagging slightly away from the corridor outside Sharma's off stump that forced him into a defensive prod, and a simple edge through to England wicket-keeper Ben Foakes. Anderson is now 3 wickets shy of joining Shane Warne and Muttiah Muralitharan in the *"700 Club"* and the third top wicket taker in the entire history of this storied game.

England added 51 runs to extend their lead on 1st innings to 353.

Joe Root remained not out on 122.

Ollie Robinson notched a maiden Test Match 50.

James Anderson delivered the prized wicket of Rohit Sharma.

India rested at the Lunch Break on 34–1 to trail by 319 runs.

It was an almost perfect morning for England.

Act Two: *Bashir turns the screw for a dominant England*

As the floodlights of the JSCA International Stadium now illuminated play beneath ever darkening skies in Ranchi dawn was breaking here in central England, and a piercing sunrise that would soon banish all traces of the bitingly cold overnight frost. A quiet and uneventful passage of play ensued, forcing the ever avuncular Graeme Swann to regale the TV audience with tales of James Anderson's good natured grumpiness amid the madness of being on tour and the superstitions that once started, can now not be broken. Run machine Yashasvi Jaiswal eased his way to 40 not out before escaping a *"catch"* that never was (despite the entire England team looking crestfallen when the TV umpire correctly declined their joyous appeal) new partner Shubman Gill had raced to 38 not out from just 65 balls received and at 86–1 on the cusp of the mid-session Drinks Break Jaiswal and Gill enjoyed a rather comfortable and unbroken partnership of 82.

Enter 20 year old Shoaib Bashir.

Rested in Rajkot, Ben Stokes clearly wanted his tall spin bowler involved early in the innings and after an hour of unbroken bowling post the Lunch Break, the 20 year old from Chertsey repaid his captain's faith with a gem of a wicket, before ripping the heart from the Indian batting order in the second hour of the session. First he trapped Shubman Gill LBW (Leg Before Wicket) with a true wonder of a delivery that I called *"out"* immediately and way before the TV umpire, a trick and treat both Bashir and I would repeat soon after as he added Rajat Patidar to his list of cricketing victims. Bashir had two brilliantly almost identical wickets, India were slowly crumbling from 86–1 to 112–3 and I clearly missed my vocation as a cricket umpire!

From a serene hour's play and accumulation of runs, Bashir had turned the session if not the Test Match on its head and on the cusp of the Tea Break he snagged the tamest of dismissals from Ravi Jadeja to leave India reeling at 131–4, still a distant 222 runs behind England on 1st innings. The only Indian batsman immune to Bashir's bewitching spell of bowling was Yashasvi Jaiswal who rested at the Tea Break 54 not out from 96 balls received. The 22 year old now has over 600 total runs in this series so far and to England's great delight today, he wouldn't add many more runs in the day's third and final session.

Act Three: *Dhruv Jurel and Kuldeep Yadav come to India's rescue*

Jaiswal added 19 further runs before becoming Bashir's 4th wicket of the innings, starting a mini batting collapse of sorts, as well as unluckily highlighting the precarious nature of this Ranchi wicket. *"The defences of Jaiswal have been broken"* proclaimed Nick Knight on TV commentary and they had, but a large slice of luck resides in Bashir's delivery barely bouncing before catching an under edge from Jaiswal's bat and back onto his stumps behind him. England had indeed broken the defences of their hosts and with India sliding from 161–4 to 171–6 and 177–7 they were in serious jeopardy of being bowled out before the close of play and still 175+ runs behind their visitors 1st innings total.

The final session's final 2 wickets belonged to Bashir's *"spin twin"* partner Tom Hartley who was indebted to a wonderful flying and diving catch from Joe Root at 1st Slip to account for Sarfaraz Khan before he flummoxed Ravi Ashwin 6 runs later and yet another dismissal via LBW. I gave Ashwin out immediately and correctly (I did tell you I should have been an umpire!) and at 177–7 India were deep in the mire and England spinning them all out in just over 2 sessions of play.

That they didn't falls squarely upon the joint efforts of Dhruv Jurel (30 not out) and Kuldeep Yadav (17 not out) and they will return in the morning with their partnership standing at an unbroken 42 and their team 134 runs behind on 1st innings with 3 wickets in hand.

So tomorrow will begin with that always pleasing *"important first hour"* of the day and should Jurel and Yadav add significant runs to their overnight not out totals and reduce England's lead to well below 100, then we'll be approaching an even game.

But should today's headliner Shoaib Bashir add to his tally of wickets or James Anderson creep ever nearer the *"700 Club"* in the opening minutes of play, England may well have a 100 run lead on 1st innings, and a suitably dominant match position befitting the Test Match so far.

See you at 3.30am under the fullest of moons and our first cup of tea of the day?

England in a spin. India now favourites in Ranchi Test

Sunday 25th February, 2024

ENGLAND 353 all out and 145 all out
INDIA 307 all out and 40–0 *(152 runs to win)*

Oh the slings and arrows of sporting luck or cricketing destiny, of chance, history or just the plain and simple truth that it's damned hard to win a game of Test Match cricket in India. Entering day 3 in Ranchi, England were in the ascendancy after having dominated this Test Match since the middle of the afternoon on day 1.

Ending day 3 today England looked rather shell-shocked as they trooped from the field of play and are now huge underdogs to a rampant India team who thoroughly and comprehensively outplayed them all day long.

If yesterday was an almost perfect day for England, today couldn't have been this beautiful in India captain Rohit Sharma's wildest sporting dreams.

Act One: *Dhruv Jurel shines as James Anderson edges closer to history*

134 runs split the teams entering the morning session with England doggedly determined to split the obstinate overnight partnership of Dhruv Jurel and Kuldeep Yadav, wrap up the Indian batting *"tail"* and enjoy a 100 run lead on 1st innings. Jurel and Yadav reciprocated their visitors dogged determination with an attritional, low scoring hour of play that scratched 34 runs away from England's overnight lead until, right on the cusp of the mid-session break, James Anderson bowled Kuldeep Yadav for a very well played 28. Yadav had only added 11 runs this morning to his overnight not out total of 17 but crucially he'd kept his senior batting partner Dhruv Jurel company for an hour this morning and in a partnership stretching back to the middle of yesterday afternoon and a partnership that will no doubt now be looked upon as not only a game changing one but a Test Match winning one. All of which is for the future, as is James Anderson's entry into the *"700 Club"* as he now sits on 698 all-time Test Match wickets. England need their legendary bowler to smash his way into this club tomorrow morning but, this is all for the future too.

The second hour of the morning session yielded more expansive, run chasing cricket from India and strictly speaking, from their wicket-keeper batsman Dhruv Jurel.

Resuming on his overnight total of 30 not out, the 23 year old from Agra reached his maiden Test Match 50 from 96 balls received before granted a *"life"* on 59 when Ollie Robinson couldn't snaffle a hard head high bullet that burst through his fingers and was only truly defeated when, on 90 and just 10 runs from a maiden Test Match century, he was bowled by a real *"Jaffa"* of a spinning delivery from Tom Hartley. 10 runs short or not from his personal milestone, Jurel had anchored the innings of his ailing team brilliantly to be the last man out in a total of 307 to trail England on 1st innings by just 46 runs.

This was India's morning and I'd argue the first session they'd *"won"* since the opening 2 hours of this Test Match. Four and a half hours later they'd won every session of the day and there was a newly installed favourite for victory in this 4th Test Match.

Act Two: *Ashwin and Yadav put England in a spin*

I've watched Test Match cricket (and always the longer form of the game as I grew up watching Test cricket with loving parents who indulged my sporting passions) for over four decades now and so I've seen my fair share of England batting collapses to know when one is in the offing. Truth be told, for the second Test Match running England have been in a dominant match winning position only to be *"skittled"* and collapse out of sight.

No slur on the ridiculous *"Bazball"* moniker or criticisms of the players themselves as quite simply, for the second match running, they've been totally and completely outplayed on cricket's crucial *"Moving Day"*.

India captain Rohit Sharma opted for spin from both ends with Ravi Ashwin and Ravi Jadeja bowling brilliantly in tandem until Ashwin dealt England a double blow in just his 3rd over. *"2 in 2 for Ravi Ashwin"* shrieked the ever excitable and exuberant legendary spin bowler Ravi Shastri on TV co-commentary and excited he rightfully was. Ashwin first snagged a limp defensive shot from Ben Duckett easily into the hands of Sarfaraz Khan at the close-in *"Bat/Pad"* position before ripping through Ollie Pope's defence with a brilliant quicker ball that trapped him dead in front of his stumps. 19–0 had become 19–2 in the blink of an eye. England's strongest part of the day was also a prelude to another horrendous dismissal for captain Ben Stokes on the cusp of the Tea Break, the wicket of Jonny Bairstow from the very first ball after the break in play and a total collapse from thereon in. Zak Crawley was England's one true light with the bat but he succumbed to the spin bowling of Kuldeep Yadav when on 60 and after Joe Root became Ravi Ashwin's 3rd wicket of the innings and just before Kuldeep Yadav tortured Ben Stokes with another delivery that barely bounced, ricocheted into the England captain's pads, before slowly tumbling onto his stumps.

It was the final ball before the Tea Break and England had recovered to 65–2 and 110–4 but at 120–5 were collapsing, and only holding an overall lead of 164 runs.

Act Three: *We have a new favourite in Ranchi*

Having completed the hard yards of getting himself in and *"set"* pre the break in play and resting at Tea 30 not out, Jonny Bairstow chipped a simple catch to Rajat Patidar from Ravi Jadeja's very first ball of the session and although Ben Foakes inched his way to 17 from 76 balls the team around him collapsed to 145 all out. Foakes was Ashwin's 4th victim and a superb delivery that forced a leading edge straight back to the champion bowler before 3 balls later James Anderson edged a catch into the juggling hands of Dhruv Jurel behind the stumps to wrap up England's innings and a tame collapse from 110–3 to 145 all out. Ashwin's final figures of 5 wickets for 51 runs was his 35th Test Match 5 wicket haul and almost certainly a match winning one.

Set 192 runs for victory, Indian openers Rohit Sharma (24) and Yashasvi Jaiswal (16 not out) cantered their way to 40 untroubled runs in the day's final 25 minutes of play to set up a final day's run chase tomorrow of 152. England captain Ben Stokes opted to bowl spin from both ends in the 8 overs bowled, leaving all-time great James Anderson to patrol the outfield.

The logic is understood but the execution from his spin bowlers was wayward and easy pickings for Sharma and Jaiswal and whereas Sharma could call upon a trio of vastly experienced spin bowlers, Stokes opted for the part-time *"Golden Arm"* of Joe Root and his two youthful inexperienced spinners. Surely Anderson was worth a 4 over burst with Sharma and Jaiswal just happy to defend until tomorrow morning? Then again, if I was England captain I'd have Anderson bowling all day from one end whilst Ian Botham, Stuart Broad, Derek Underwood and Bob Willis bowled in strict rotation from the other. What England would give for Bob Willis tomorrow morning, bustling in, the wind in his hair, fire in his nostrils, desperate for a victory from the jaws of almost certain defeat.

England commenced day 3 with a 134 run lead and in as dominant a position as you could wish for, and deservedly so.

India ended day 3 chasing a further 152 runs to win after an incredible day saw them outplay England in every cricketing department.

We have a new favourite for victory in Ranchi.

India too strong for plucky England in Ranchi

Monday 26th February, 2024

ENGLAND 353 all out and 145 all out
INDIA 307 all out and 192–5

India win by 5 wickets

OK I admit I got more than a little excited when 20 year old spinning sensation Shoaib Bashir snagged the consecutive wickets of Ravi Jadeja and Sarfaraz Khan to reduce India to 120–5 and still 72 runs shy of their victory target. England had chipped away all morning without any real tangible return and India were just 108 runs from taking a deserved 3–1 lead in this best of 5 series. Then a brilliant, game changing passage of play saw England eating *"dessert after their lunch"* according to Ravi Shastri, and the national team he decorated with his presence as both player and coach had collapsed from 99–1 to 120–5 either side of the Lunch Break, and as dawn was slowly breaking here in central England, I was reaching for another pack of chocolate biscuits.

And why not?

England were back in a game they were winning handsomely at the start of play yesterday only to be rank underdogs come the end of a chastening day. It's the flow of the Test Match tides. So dominant to being so outplayed in a matter of a few sporting hours beneath India's darkest of skies. England's *"Golden Arm"* Joe Root accounted for Yashasvi Jaiswal before Tom Hartley bamboozled Rohit Sharma into a *"double dismissal"* as he was both caught AND stumped, a very rare and very pleasing oddity in this grandest of all games, before Shoaib Bashir dismissed Rajat Patidar courtesy of a flying reactionary catch from Ollie Pope and at the Lunch Break, England had cause for hope to spring eternal.

Two quick wickets from the spinning fingers of 20 year old Shoaib Bashir greeted the resumption of play after the Lunch Break, and with England enjoying their post lunch desserts and India still needing 72 further runs to win, I was getting all rather excited and opening yet another pack of chocolate biscuits.

What?

You should have seen the breaking of a dawn of a brand new day that I was witnessing, a red and purple haze hovering in the near distance and above an isolated hill of local renown known as *"The Wrekin"*. The confusion of colours had replaced the blackest of nights under a star filled sky and in the presence and the madness of an (almost) full moon.

Watching Test Match cricket through the night doesn't tend to afford you the luxury of sleep and after 4 consecutive, albeit self-imposed nights of little to no sleep the walls begin to bend, you start seeing unique forms of losing your wicket I'd have LOVED explaining to my dear old Test Match cricket loving Mum, and this England team never fails to give you a reason to believe. With dawn breaking and a fresh cup of tea resting beside a newly opened pack of chocolate biscuits India were 120–5 and still 72 runs short of victory. From nowhere, England were now 5 wickets from victory themselves, very much back in a Test Match flowing on those beautifully unpredictable tides, and I was still a believer.

Alas England lost a second Test Match in a row whereby they were thoroughly outplayed in the crucial crossover into the 3rd innings, an occasion often crowned as *"Moving Day"*. They lost both, spectacularly, both here and in Rajkot, and both whilst holding the whip hand in the contest. There will be no outlandish slurs cast on the way these revolutionaries play the game, and especially not here as once again they were outplayed in crucial phases of the game by an almost unbeatable India on their home turf. This was another mature performance in many ways, and far away from the *"Bazball"* media creation.

Joe Root scored a tremendous century.

The team as a whole compiled an above par 1st innings total and whilst they were frustrated not to end the Indian innings sooner and with a bigger lead, they began yesterday as firm favourites only to end it 8 hours later miles behind and needing snookers.

The flowing tides of Test Match cricket rather swept England away.

To the victors belong the spoils and even a much changed India missing a backbone of national cricketing stars are still near unbeatable in home conditions. They have found a new wicket-keeper batsman in today's headline hero Dhruv Jurel. His calming 39 not out from 77 balls received perfectly accompanied the steady ship sailed by Shubman Gill on his way to 52 from 124 balls and another performance submitted for his permanent place as India's number 3 batsman.

Rohit Sharma isn't going anywhere, or at least I hope he isn't, and surely he'll be invigorated further to continue playing into his 40s if only to open the batting with his team's bright young thing, Yashasvi Jaiswal.

Welcome back a fully fit and happy Virat Kohli in front of Ravi Jadeja and Sarfaraz Khan (both desperate for their respective batting slots) today's headliner Dhruv Jurel at 7 ahead of Ravi Ashwin and Kuldeep Yadav and returning superstar Jasprit Bumrah replacing Mohammed Siraj, and India are putting together a team to compete in the here and now as well as the foreseeable future.

I've penned this journal entry with an end of tour feeling yet we have one final Test Match to look forward to in Dharamshala. Sometimes you just have to float on the cricketing tides. After four long nights under a full moon anything is possible. I predicted 4-1 India at the start of the tour whilst hoping for an exciting 3-2 England defeat. So providing the game isn't abandoned due to rain or snow (yes, snow in India!) or a cricketing draw (unlikely with these teams) I'll be a cricketing sage one way or the other come the middle of March.

"We didn't have a chance in hell of even competing with India, but even today that wasn't an easy win for India and I think they would admit that" proclaimed a proud Ben Stokes immediately after his team's defeat. *"I'm very proud of the way every player has thrown everything at India. No-one has ever taken a backward step."* Nor will they in Dharamshala where Rohit Sharma will await with an eager, confident, developing team desperate for another Test Match victory.

The key word Sharma reiterated in his post-match interviews was *"hunger"* and *"there's no point playing those who do not have the hunger"*, a pointed reference to the vast amount of cricket available and a desire to keep Test Match cricket sacrosanct. *"The thing with Test cricket is that you get very few opportunities. If you don't utilise them, they go away"*.

Kuldeep Yadav spins England out of control in Dharamshala

Thursday 7th March, 2024

ENGLAND 218 all out
INDIA 135–1 *(trailing by 83 runs)*

At 100–1 on the cusp of the Lunch Break, England had *"won"* the opening session of this fifth and final Test Match in the foothills of the Himalayas and were in almost complete control in beautiful Dharamshala. Two hours after the resumption in play after the first official break for the day they'd crumbled and collapsed under the weight of an incredible spell of mystery spin bowling from 29 year old Kuldeep Yadav and already face an arduous task to simply stay competitive in this Test Match. But that's getting ahead of ourselves.

First we have the good news that your favourite cricket correspondent is the toast of the town and his new cricket club's debut hero!

Despite an afternoon spent ambling along the River Severn in central England and admiring the oldest iron bridge in the whole wide world, I simply couldn't sleep last evening.

This is nothing new and after struggling for what seemed like an entire Test Match series to finally find the peace and solace of the sleep world I was startled awake by the shrill of a 3.30am alarm and from a dreamworld whereby I was a local hero once more. Dreams are strange beasts aren't they? For at 3.29am I was walking around the boundary rope at my new cricket club a match winning hero and I distinctly remember, upon the shrill of that damn alarm, admiring the scoreboard and *"Stephen Blackford 18 Not Out"* illuminated for all to see. After taking a bagful of wickets on day one of our four day game (amateurs such as myself rarely if ever play multiple day games), my new team had matched the opposition's 1st innings score on day two before on day three I had no doubt matched my day one feat of grabbing a bucketful of wickets once again. I don't remember this part of the dream but as the hero of my own story, let's go with it.

So onto day four and chasing a relatively modest target for victory my new team had collapsed in their run chase for victory leaving a teammate and myself batting in my usual slot of number 11 to grab victory from the jaws of certain defeat. 18 undefeated runs later, my teammate and I are chaired from the field of play before freshly showered and strolling around the boundary edge after the match. I can't help but smile at the scoreboard, my individual achievement and my team's last gasp victory.

Then the alarm dragged me wearily and sleepily back into the real world.

Dreams are strange beasts aren't they?

Act One: *England win the opening session. Just.*

After winning the toss at the almost universally agreed most beautiful setting for a cricket ground in all the world, the snow capped mountains of the Himalayas a perfect backdrop behind the vibrant red coloured Pavilion and multi coloured seats of the HPCA Stadium, England captain Ben Stokes had no hesitation whatsoever in deciding to bat first on a wicket described by ex England spin bowler Graeme Swann as a *"belter"* of a wicket for batting.

On the milestone occasion of 100 Test Matches for both Ravi Ashwin and Jonny Bairstow, the predicted sleet and snow had not materialised and whilst unseasonably cold for players and a huge contingent from England who had flown in especially for this Test Match and the exploration of the nearby hills and mountains, I quickly wrapped myself in a warming duvet with my first cup of tea of the morning, a chocolate biscuit or three and enjoyed a masterclass of pure batting style, technique and run accumulation from England opener, Zak Crawley.

Whilst opening partner Ben Duckett rather *"scratched around"* before finally finding his feet and then surrendering his wicket to a magnificent running catch from Shubman Gill that presented Kuldeep Yadav his first wicket of 5 today, Crawley survived a close TV umpire review when on 29 in an otherwise faultless and dominating 50 run partnership with Duckett (their 5th such partnership of the series) before surviving another TV review when on 38, reaching his half century from 64 balls received before resting at the Lunch Break 61 not out. I have long championed Crawley's ability, upright and *"correct"* batting style and I marvelled at a beautiful 2 hour's of batting from the 26 year old from Bromley in Kent. He continues to be England's top run scorer during this tour with his 4th 50+ score and 14th overall in a Test Match career that with the avoidance of injury can only soar into the stratosphere in the coming decade and more.

The same can be said for England's number 3 Ollie Pope but today, he rather let his team down and from his downfall onward, England spiralled quickly to collapse.

First things first, Pope was beaten by a beauty of a delivery from Kuldeep Yadav when on 11 that saw him stumped by Dhruv Jurel and the England vice-captain yards out of his crease.

It was a beauty of a delivery.

But with the clock ticking down to the Lunch Break and mere seconds from this 40 minute break in play, surely Pope should have simply, in the cricketing vernacular, *"shut up shop"* for the break, not *"danced down the wicket"*, and rather taken his 11 not out runs with him and rested comfortably beside Crawley at Lunch and their team 100–1. That would have been an almost perfect morning for the visitors.

Instead, a rush of blood to the head saw England winning the opening session, just, but 100–2 was much more of an even outcome as England once more had a match in this series in their dominating grasp and 2 hours of play later, they'd be tumbling to complete collapse once more.

Act Two: *Kuldeep Yadav spins England to distraction*

For 37 runs in the afternoon session, Zak Crawley and new partner Joe Root serenely accumulated a burgeoning partnership that saw Crawley gifted an extra *"life"* when on 61 and India captain Rohit Sharma refusing to acquiesce to the adamant appeals from Sarfaraz Khan at the *"Short Leg"* position that he'd feathered a tiny edge into his scampering, scrambling and diving hands. He had.

Crawley played a batsman's poker face. Sharma refused to refer it to the TV umpire, and the young man escaped with his wicket intact.

But as I and Graeme Swann dreamed of a dominant century that would set England on the way to a huge 1st innings total, Kuldeep Yadav had other ideas with another of those beautiful spinning deliveries that pitched around Crawley's off stump before spinning through his advancing attacking shot and crashing into his leg stump. *"The brilliance of Kuldeep Yadav"* exclaimed Swann before a crushing summing up of *"It won't be a century for Crawley"*. The England opening batsman had once again scored a half century, had once again advanced into the 70's (79) and England were once again on the road to a humiliating batting collapse.

The onset of the collapse followed a brief, quick fire and thrilling 38 run partnership between Jonny Bairstow and Joe Root but Bairstow's departure for a rapid 29 from just 18 balls received left England 175–4 and just 12 deliveries later, they were 175–6 having added zero to their innings total and losing both their past and present captains in the process. Ravi Jadeja accounted for Joe Root by brilliantly trapping him *"dead"* and *"plumb"* in front of his stumps for a resiliently made 26 before Kuldeep Yadav repeated the exact same trick, and even more spectacularly, to dismiss current captain Ben Stokes for a *"duck"*. 8 team runs later saw the departure of Tom Hartley and Mark Wood in the space of 3 balls and England, so dominant at 100–1 on the cusp of the Lunch Break, were collapsing on the cusp of the Tea Break at 183–8.

In under 2 hours of play England had lost the heart of their batting order to Kuldeep Yadav and now half of their batting *"tail"* to Ravi Ashwin for a paltry 83 runs.

Act Three: *India pile on the misery for a bamboozled England*

England reached the Tea Break on 194–8 before being indebted on the resumption of play to a 35 run partnership between Ben Foakes and Shoaib Bashir that ended cruelly for Foakes and then the innings entire for England, and 218 all out. Foakes unluckily *"played on"* to his stumps after scoring 24 before Ravi Ashwin wrapped up the innings with his 4th wicket just 3 balls later by dismissing James Anderson and England hadn't so much been bowled out but, if you'll permit me, been bamboozled out by the mystery spin of Kuldeep Yadav (5 wickets for 72 runs from 15 overs) and Test Match celebrating centurion Ravi Ashwin (4 wickets for 51 runs from 11 overs).

Kuldeep Yadav had ripped the heart from the England batting order.

Ravi Ashwin had mopped up the tail.

England had collapsed from 100–1 to 218 all out on a *"belter"* of a wicket.

Any hopes of James Anderson and Mark Wood repeating the trick with the new ball of Indian counterparts Jasprit Bumrah and Mohammed Siraj by bowling difficult to score tight, swinging and seaming deliveries quickly evaporated in 7 rather uneventful overs before Indian opening batsmen Rohit Sharma and Yashasvi Jaiswal smashed their way to a century opening partnership in just 20 overs. Although Jaiswal perished soon after for a run-a-ball 57, captain Sharma remains not out overnight on 52 and accompanied by Shubman Gill will return in the morning with their team just 83 runs adrift on 1st innings and unless England have a dream opening session tomorrow, India will be far ahead and over the Himalayan mountains and into the cricketing distance come the Tea Break tomorrow afternoon.

England need a dream morning.

I wonder what dreams I have in store for me later.

I sure hope they're far sexier than last night's version!

See you tomorrow.

India are over the Himalayan Mountains and far, far away

Friday 8th March, 2024

ENGLAND 218 all out
INDIA 473–8 *(leading by 255 runs)*

I concluded yesterday's journal with a very simple statement positing that England needed a *"dream"* morning session lest they be batted out of a competitive contest. Alas, rather than the dream scenario of snagging a bagful of quick Indian wickets they in fact experienced a humbling nightmare of a morning that began a day of vastly fluctuating fortunes for both teams but which ultimately ended with the hosts in an entirely expected dominant position entering day 3 tomorrow.

But as ever we're getting ahead of ourselves and we must start, as we shall for the remainder of this Test Match in the foothills of the Himalayan mountains, 7,000 miles away in the down under sunshine of Christchurch, New Zealand.

Act One: *Step forward your Centurions*

With sleep evading my grasp once more it was an easy decision to warm up for the cold, snow capped mountains of the Himalayas with first the opening two sessions of the 2nd Test Match between the Kiwis of New Zealand and their noisy cousins Australia from the other side of the Tasman Sea. The duly crowned World Test Champion Australia team have long been the undoubted best Test Match cricket playing team in the world regardless of their crown and once again they proved their sporting point in devastating fashion.

Already leading this 2 match series 1–0, Aussie captain Pat Cummins won the toss and immediately inserted his hosts into bat on a typically New Zealand *"green seamer"* of a bowler friendly wicket. Whilst this decision originally appeared to be backfiring as Kiwi openers Tom Latham and Will Young batted comfortably and largely untroubled for nearly 90 minutes, Young's departure for 14 was soon followed by his opening partner for a well made 38 and then, right on the cusp of the Lunch Break, bright young thing Rachin Ravindra surrendered his wicket for just 4 and Aussie fast bowler supreme Josh Hazlewood had secured the first 2 of his overall 5 wicket haul to come.

New Zealand sporting hero Kane Williamson, celebrating his 100th Test Match in tandem with his captain Tim Southee, would disappoint a sell-out Christchurch crowd in the forever beautiful *"Hagley Oval"* with just 17 runs before becoming Hazlewood's 4th victim shortly after the departure of big hitting Daryl Mitchell and from 47-0, the Kiwis had collapsed to 84-5. The hosts would roughly double this total to a limp 162 all out and had it not been for a last wicket stand of defiance and a crucial 55 run partnership between captain Southee and Matt Henry, the hosts could have crumbled all out just past the 100 run mark.

It was at this point in Christchurch that I crossed to those snow capped mountains of the Himalayas but suffice to say and rather predictably, Australia ended the day a couple of hours later on 124-4 to trail their hosts by just 38 runs on 1st innings, with Marnus Labuschagne, one part of my affectionately self-titled *"Chuckle Brothers"* with Steve Smith, finally finding form with the bat to return in the morning 45 not out.

So from the number one Test Match playing team in the world we travel 7,000 miles to arguably the team determined to wrest away their crown.

Commencing this morning on a commanding 135–1 and trailing England on 1st innings by just 83 runs, India, in the guise of their captain Rohit Sharma (52 not out) and Shubman Gill (26 not out) started as they meant to go on with terrific gusto and by dismantling the opening bowling from James Anderson and Shoaib Bashir with boundary 4's and boundary clearing 6's aplenty. Whilst England appeared *"Punch Drunk"* according to the ever entertaining ex England spin bowler Graeme Swann, Gill was quickly playing catch up with his senior skipper and partner Sharma as he raced to his half century from just 64 balls received and at the mid-session break for drinks, India had reached 202–1 and had added a quick-fire 67 runs in total without losing any wickets.

This painful pattern for England would continue throughout the second hour of play this morning as first Sharma (100 from 160 balls received) and then Gill (100 from 142 balls received) each reached their century milestone whilst adding a further 62 team runs in the hour's play to rest at the Lunch Break with each a Test Match century under their belts and unbeaten, and a 1st innings team total of 264–1. In this morning session alone each batsman had reached their century, the 1st innings scores between the teams were level after just 80 minutes of play, 129 total runs were added without the loss of any wickets and at Lunch, India already had a commanding lead on 1st innings of 46 runs with 9 wickets still in hand and 2 batsmen resting on centuries.

Act Two: *Who writes Ben Stokes' scripts?*

This session of two very distinct halves started with a *"magic ball"*, a *"fantasy"*, a cricketing *"Jaffa"* or just an absolute beauty of a delivery from Ben Stokes that pitched on middle stump before jagging perfectly past the forward defence of Rohit Sharma to crash spectacularly into his off stump. The Indian captain and centurion had added just a single run to his pre Lunch century before receiving the archetypal unplayable delivery from his opposite number but what was far more remarkable and fitting for this cricketing fantasy was that this delivery, this first ball from Ben Stokes, was his first ball bowled in anger since last Summer and since a self-imposed ban from bowling to aid his recovery from a knee injury that, fingers crossed, can now finally be banished to the mists of a former time. Despite delivering a quite unplayable delivery that crashed into his opposite number's off stump, Stokes barely registered any kind of celebration whatsoever but rather left it to his great mates Mark Wood, James Anderson and coach Brendon McCullum to sum up this somewhat unreal turn of events by simply smiling in astonishment and holding their heads in shocked wonder.

Sharma returned to the Pavilion smiling broadly for he had been utterly defeated and no doubt wondered to himself who indeed wrote Ben Stokes' scripts!

The script writers were clearly busy in Dharamshala as just 4 runs and 7 deliveries later, James Anderson followed his captain's lead by bowling another beauty *"through the gate"* of Shubman Gill's defence to dismantle his *"castle"* of stumps behind him, ripping his off stump clean from the ground in the process. Both centurions had been dismissed in a matter of minutes, India had finally been reduced from 275–1 to 279–3 but far more notably, James Anderson had his 699th Test Match wicket to stand on the cusp of joining the vaunted *"700 Club"* and becoming only its third member in the entire storied history of this magnificent game.

The afternoon session of two very differing halves was now underway in earnest and in the hands of yet another debutant for India in this series as well as a fellow newbie playing only his 3rd Test Match for his country. Thrust together at 279–3, the very impressive Sarfaraz Khan ostensibly received a *"life"* when on just 2 with Ben Stokes disappointing his script writers by dropping a return catch off his own bowling only to raise his hands in praise to the heavens when discovering he'd bowled a *"no ball"*. By the mid-session break for drinks, Khan had carefully edged and crafted his way to 8 not out. In contrast, debut maker Devdutt Padikkal arrived at a Test Match crease for the first time and, in the cricketing vernacular, *"only dealt in boundaries"* as he raced to 31 not out with 28 coming from sparkling boundary 4's.

The roles were then reversed in the second hour of the session with Padikkal far more circumspect as he added just 13 runs to be 44 not out at the Tea Break whilst his partner, in an on-going unbroken partnership of 97, raced from 8 to a run-a-ball 51 not out, their team total to 376-3 and a lead on 1st innings of 158 runs.

Act Three: *Shoaib Bashir leads England fightback*

The day's final session was a beautiful mix of fluctuating fortunes and perfectly representative of everything that came before it.

Yet again we had a wicket straight after the resumption in play as Shoaib Bashir spun a gem of a delivery that Sarfaraz Khan could only edge and help its way into the eager hands of Joe Root at 1st Slip, Devdutt Padikkal reached his milestone maiden Test Match half century before being utterly defeated by another gem of a spinning delivery from Shoaib Bashir and Dhruv Jurel *"holed out"* on the boundary for just 15 to present the ever eager and impressive Bashir with his 4th wicket of the innings.

The tumble of quick wickets continued via the spinning fingers of his partner Tom Hartley as he snagged both Ravi Jadeja and Ravi Ashwin in the space of 5 deliveries to become the top wicket taker of the series with 22 before, with England smelling sporting blood for the first time in the match, Kuldeep Yadav and Jasprit Bumrah resisted everything the visitors could throw at them in an unbroken stand of 45 that ensured India reached the day ending "*Stumps*" on 473–8 and a huge, dare I say unbeatable lead on 1st innings of 255 runs.

So that was the day that was.

India compiled 338 runs on the day for the loss of 7 wickets to enter day 3 with a lead of 255 runs and counting.

England's impossible mission is a simple one on paper, but rather more daunting when under the spectre of those snow covered mountains of the Himalayas and in the face of the bowling attack of Jasprit Bumrah, Kuldeep Yadav, Ravi Ashwin and Ravi Jadeja: They first need to dismiss India's final 2 wickets quickly for the addition of next to zero runs before scoring at least 255+ runs to make their hosts bat again AND score at least 450 2nd innings runs to make this Test Match a competitive affair.

There are 3 days left in this Test Match but they need to resurrect the spirit of Hyderabad, find a couple of century makers and even that may not be enough without the assistance of Tom Cruise and perhaps even an Exorcist.

See you in the morning!

Anderson the record breaker but Ashwin spins England to defeat

Saturday 9th March, 2024

ENGLAND 218 all out and 195 all out
INDIA 477 all out

India win by an Innings and 64 runs

My winter odyssey is over.

No more shrills from an alarm clock at 3.30am to shake me from a dreamworld that seems more real than our upside down world with every passing day. The revolutionaries from England have been well and truly humbled and dare I say that I predicted the eventual series score of 4–1 to India? Perhaps not or more accurately not again and certainly not in the raw aftermath of yet another comprehensive defeat in the Ben Stokes and Brendon McCullum reinvention of English cricket. As ever, there will be no overall criticism of the absurd media moniker of *"Bazball"* as the cold, hard truth is that England faced the toughest touring assignment in Test Match cricket and were thoroughly bested and beaten by an Indian team who rarely if ever lose a series on home soil.

The lasting worry as a fan and obsessive writer on this grandest of all games is the margin of the 4 individual defeats and how they've escalated from a tight English victory in the first Test to defeats by 106 runs, an incredible 434 runs, 5 wickets and today a thumping innings and 64 runs.

Thankfully for all concerned this isn't a worry I have to carry for long and will soon become the sole preserve of Messrs Stokes and McCullum and in their safe hands the future of English Test Match cricket will continue to be curated in their revolutionary grasp. From Pakistan to New Zealand, the drawn Ashes battle with Australia through to this new year tour of India, it's been a hell of a ride and as with the drawn series with the two down under nations they've had major opportunities in India to exploit dominating positions into winning Test Matches. Please don't mistake this for my saying that England could have won this series. That would be absurd considering the 4–1 score line. But individual and team mistakes have cost them yet again and during these past weeks of an Indian Summer, they've proven far more costly than a one run defeat to New Zealand this time last year and the agony of a drawn series with their neighbours Australia this past Summer that should have seen Stokes and McCullum's charges triumphant in a come from behind Ashes win for the ages.

During today's immediate post-match TV interview Stokes was honest enough to admit his team had been **"outplayed by the better team over the series"** and expressed his excitement to **"drive the team forward"** through their home Summer encounters with both the West Indies and Sri Lanka as well as lamenting that his team needed to be more **"relentless"** in key moments to turn series draws and defeats into the ultimate destination of Test Match wins. He was effusive in his praise of the opening batting partnership of Zak Crawley and Ben Duckett before being unable to hide his glowing admiration for his three youthful spin bowlers in the guise of Rehan Ahmed, Shoaib Bashir and Tom Hartley as well as lavishing praise on record breaker James Anderson who in his words is the role model for every aspiring fast bowler to **"look up to"** and **"as fit as I've ever seen him"** and determined to continue playing as he approaches his frankly astounding quarter of a century of continuous play at the highest level his sport has to offer.

The Stokes and McCullum revolution still has a long way to go as they strive relentlessly forward for the consistency of performance that will surely see their team secure future series wins. They have a settled and successful opening partnership of Zak Crawley and Ben Duckett with Crawley the team's top run scorer on the tour with 407 runs and the partnership enjoying 5 opening stands of 50+ runs or more.

Despite his match winning century in Hyderabad it's been a rather sketchy tour for number 3 and vice-captain Ollie Pope but he remains a mainstay of this team ahead of Joe Root at number 4 with the Yorkshireman ending the tour in fine form with a century in Ranchi, a combined 110 runs here in Dharamshala and 320 runs across the 5 match series. The number 5 batting position is a contentious affair with Jonny Bairstow getting several starts but no big scores and with fellow Yorkshireman Harry Brook waiting in the wings and sure to return, either Bairstow calls time on his Test Match career having reached a century of matches or he replaces the continually unlucky and under pressure Ben Foakes at number 7 and the other side of his captain in the batting order.

This leaves Stokes and McCullum with the juggling act of finding a place in their team for their number one spin bowler Jack Leach with three young spin bowlers breathing down his neck, and a possible return to the fold of Chris Woakes in a fast bowling attack seemingly to contain the evergreen 41 year old record breaker James Anderson and one other. Mark Wood, a personal favourite of mine, is 34 years old but as fast as ever and whilst Ollie Robinson is never going to be the answer due to injury and a complete lack of enthusiasm for the toil of Test Match cricket, Gus Atkinson and Josh Tongue might be.

As mentioned above, thankfully for all concerned these worries and decisions are not mine, but the Stokes and McCullum revolution will always have me in their corner come what may.

Winning captain Rohit Sharma and coach Rahul Dravid have a similar if vastly more positive selection headache ahead of their mouth watering encounter with Australia later in the year as through circumstance, injury and pure sporting desire, they have a nailed on opening batting partner for Rohit Sharma in the guise of *"Man of the Series"* Yashasvi Jaiswal, Shubman Gill has surely cemented his place in the team at number 3, Ravi Jadeja has equally made his case to be a permanent number 5 going forward and Sarfaraz Khan is a brilliantly talented all-rounder surely destined to bat at number 6. Before we confirm Dhruv Jurel as the team's new wicket-keeper at number 7 we must address the pleasing headaches for captain and coach alike as crowd darling Virat Kohli must surely return at number 4 and therefore a team so cruelly decimated at the beginning of this tour with his absence, and that of Rishabh Pant and KL Rahul, must now endeavour to find a place in a successful and winning team for them, let alone a returning Mohammed Shami in a team already full to the brim with Jasprit Bumrah and three world class spinners. As I say, quite the pleasing headache to have!

In his post-match TV interview Rohit Sharma addressed this pleasing quandary as *"people are going to go and people are going to come"* before extolling the virtues of an ever changing squad and starting XI with *"guys that responded well under pressure"*. He somewhat reiterated his comments from the end of the 4th Test Match: of players needing to want and desire to play this longer form of the game, to *"make a difference"*, and although runs on the board was imperative it was also *"important to take 20 wickets in Test Match cricket"*. He noted the importance of Kuldeep Yadav whilst also recognising that he was a very individual personality in a team game, Yashasvi Jaiswal has a *"long way to go"* yet also a *"tough guy"* for someone so young and he beamed with pride at now being able to fully talk openly about the 22 year old star of the series and top run scorer with a phenomenal 712 runs to his name and already over 1,000 Test Match runs in the bank after just 2 series of the red ball game.

Following the conclusion of this Test series India now sit top of the World Test Championship standings and will remain so irrespective of the final result in the two match series between New Zealand and Australia with which I'll conclude today's daily journal. But first, a return to the field of play today in Dharamshala and for 15 minutes, England had the perfect start to a day that would end so quickly and indeed so imperfectly.

For it took the visitors just a quarter of an hour and the cost of just 2 runs to snag the final 2 wickets of India's 1st Innings and for 2 distinctly different milestones for 2 England bowlers separated by an entire adult generation and still less years than James *"Jimmy"* Anderson's storied Test Match playing career. In the space of 3 balls and just as many minutes, first 41 year old James Anderson snagged the edge of Kuldeep Yadav's bat and into the safe gloved hands of Ben Foakes behind the stumps for his 700th all-time Test Match wicket to become only the third player in the entire history of the game to reach this incredible milestone, and then 20 year old Shoaib Bashir grabbed the final wicket of the innings to secure a 5 wicket haul before the old stager and the young buck led their team from the field of play with a very real sense of a job well done. England trailed India on 1st innings by a mammoth 257 runs and as a first port of call they had to bat for the remainder of the day to draw level on runs with India before setting their hosts any kind of total to chase on day 4.

Sadly, they didn't even manage to bat until Tea time.

Aside from Ben Duckett's incredibly reckless and badly judged rush down the wicket just 11 balls into the innings (only to hear the *"death rattle"* of his stumps shattering behind him), the rest of his teammates were either out-thought or out-skilled by the entire rainbow of the Indian bowling attack led brilliantly once more by Ravi Ashwin in his 100th Test Match.

The 37 year old veteran had 4 wickets to his name even before the players left the field for the Lunch Break as he followed the gift of Duckett's self-inflicted demise by brilliantly spinning out Zak Crawley for a *"duck"*, out-thinking Ollie Pope and dismantling Ben Stokes' *"castle"* of stumps. At 103-5 at Lunch, England were ripe for the easily predictable collapse that soon followed as Ashwin bowled Ben Foakes before he left the stage clear for Jasprit Bumrah to *"york"* Tom Hartley and Mark Wood in 3 devastatingly brilliant deliveries, Ravi Jadeja ended the stout defiance of Tom Hartley before the bowling rainbow was completed by Kuldeep Yadav as he secured the match winning wicket of Joe Root. Before running out of partners, the ex skipper was the only England batsman to provide any meaningful resistance with a well played 84, but the team around him had collapsed to 195 all out in less than 50 overs and in under 2 sessions of play.

England had been thoroughly and comprehensively outplayed once more.

As promised in yesterday's journal entry I'll conclude with the antipodean contest at the beautiful *"Hagley Oval"* in Christchurch, New Zealand and pleasingly and very much against the run of play, the hosts have turned the tables on their visitors from the other side of the Tasman Sea and after 2 days of this Test Match, we may have a competitive game on our hands.

Commencing day 2 on 124–4 and trailing New Zealand by just 38 1st Innings runs, Australia dominated the early exchanges with overnight *"Night Watchman"* Nathan Lyon granted a *"life"* just 8 deliveries into the day with Daryl Mitchell dropping a tough chance at 2nd Slip before snagging an almost exact replica 30 minutes and 19 runs to the emergency batsman later. Mitchell Marsh soon followed for a 4 ball *"duck"* (Matt Henry's 5th wicket of the innings) before the *"Golden Arm"* of part-time bowler Glenn Phillips snagged a loose shot from Alex Carey with his very first delivery. Australia had matched and surpassed New Zealand's 1st innings total to lead by 27 runs at the fall of Carey's wicket and would extend this lead by a further 32 runs when, right on the cusp of the Lunch Break, Glenn Phillips was back in the action with as spectacular a catch as you could wish to see, flying to his right goalkeeper style to snag a quite wonderful one-handed catch to see the back of Aussie danger man and top scorer Marnus Labuschagne 10 runs short of a deserved Test Match century.

New Zealand needed just 35 minutes of the afternoon session to wrap up the remainder of the Australian innings and had it not been for a blistering run-a-ball 23 from Aussie captain Pat Cummins, they would have done so much sooner and with a far lesser deficit on 1st innings than the eventual 94 runs behind they found themselves with starting their 2nd Innings.

Both of the final 2 wickets to fall were snagged by Matt Henry who took his pre-Lunch tally of 5 wickets to 7 and a second best personal bowling figures of his Test Match career of 7–67. I continued watching live until turning my undivided attention to Dharamshala, leaving New Zealand on 79–1, 15 runs behind their visitors, and with opening batsman Tom Latham 38 not out and all around Kiwi sporting hero Kane Williamson 36 not out. Highlights of the 90 minutes or so of live play missed show Latham receiving a *"life"* when inexplicably dropped by the gloved hands of wicket-keeper Alex Carey when on 59 (he remains 65 not out) before the sell-out Christchurch crowd cried out in anguish with the departure of Kane Williamson for 51 as he *"played on"* to his own stumps from the bowling of Pat Cummins. Rachin Ravindra (11 not out) joined Tom Latham until the day ending *"Stumps"* minutes later, and New Zealand will resume in the morning to another sell-out Sunday crowd in the Christchurch sunshine on 134–2 and with a lead of 40 runs.

So my attention now turns permanently to New Zealand for hopefully an exciting and competitive final chapter to my winter odyssey and if I'm lucky, and because I adore this grandest of all games so much, maybe two final chapters.

Time will tell.

It always does.

Aussies "possums in the headlights" as Kiwis chase for victory

New Zealand v Australia, 10th March 2024

NEW ZEALAND 162 all out and 372 all out
AUSTRALIA 256 all out and 77–4 *(needing 202 runs to win)*

Last evening as the floodlights of the *"Hagley Oval"* began to replace the setting sun across this beautifully quaint cricket ground a world away from the cold and rain of an English winter, Kiwi batsmen Tom Latham and Rachin Ravindra were, in the cricketing vernacular, *"jumping around"* as they battled valiantly to repel everything their Australian counterparts could throw and indeed bowl at them. This evening the roles were reversed after yet another of those quite astounding days that only Test Match cricket can provide and now Australia were not only jumping around to avoid the searing deliveries from an inspired Matt Henry and debutant Ben Sears they were *"possums in the headlights"* according to ex Kiwi international Mark Richardson and at 34–4, threatening to crumble and collapse to defeat on New Zealand soil for the first time in 31 years.

We're getting ahead of ourselves again as we always do but after another night of watching cricket through the night and against the the perceived pun intended boundaries of the time matrix the walls are beginning to bend as they are oft to do, today's final chapter of a winter's watching cricket from the other side of the world has a pleasing extra edition to follow later today and a day here in England celebrated as *"Mother's Day"* and boy do I miss a mother who so adored this grandest of all games. It's 7.11am as I pen these words on a cold and rainy English Sunday morning. The birds are chirping their early morning songs of praise and salutations. The beloved Reds of my Liverpool footballing heart are sure to have their bubble pricked if not popped entirely by the Champions of the World later today and I'm missing a grand old lady who through her love of cricket introduced me to this wonderful sport what seems like a lifetime ago. Three years in the time matrix feels as long as a night time of watching cricket through the night, two months of watching cricket through the night in fact, and we're getting ahead of ourselves and travelling back in time, mixing our sporting metaphors and allegiances, thinking of a Manchester United fan who will be willing my team defeat her cousins from the other side of Manchester later today and after which, I'll have one last dance with the midnight devil of watching Test Match cricket through the night and for that, we should all be truly thankful.

So where were we?

After battling and indeed batting valiantly last evening to preserve their wickets, Tom Latham (65 not out) and Rachin Ravindra (11 not out) resumed this morning with their Kiwi team total standing on 134–2 and with a precious lead entering day 3 of 40 runs. Although Latham would fall just 25 minutes into the day's play for the addition of just 8 runs to his total, the bright young thing beside him became the mainstay of a New Zealand 2nd innings that threatened at one stage to completely bat Australia out of the contest but which, pleasingly for an English neutral on the other side of the world, perfectly set up a difficult but attainable run chase for victory of 279.

We're getting ahead of ourselves once more so returning to this morning and as the clock ticked past the witching hour of midnight here in England, Rachin Ravindra remained unbeaten at one end whilst the loud and brilliantly brash Daryl Mitchell joined him at the other in a partnership of 123 that truly threatened to end any Aussie hopes of victory.

Mitchell finally departed for 58 after reaching his 10th all-time Test Match half-century and first against Australia and although Ravindra would follow him back to the Pavilion just 9 balls later for a priceless 82 from 153 balls received, the 24 year old wunderkind had provided the backbone and platform for the innings that would see both Glenn Phillips and Matt Henry chipping in with 16 valuable runs each as well as a run-a-ball cameo innings of 44 from an injured Scott Kuggeleijn that saw him granted not one but two extra *"lives"* before he *"holed out"* chasing a half-century and the last wicket to fall in a 2nd innings team total of 372 that set their Australian visitors from across the Tasman Sea 279 runs for victory.

Australia now had two hours to bat in front of a packed and sold out Christchurch crowd and from 15-0 they collapsed to 34-4 in just 45 minutes and 7 thrilling overs of bowling from Matt Henry seeking a career high 10 total wickets in a Test Match for the first time and 26 year old debutant Ben Sears. Henry struck first, trapping the dangerous and soon to be Hall of Fame legend Steve Smith *"plumb"* LBW in front of his stumps for just 9 before his great mate Marnus Labuschagne was granted a *"life"* 7 balls later when dropped by Daryl Mitchell at 2nd Slip before departing just 2 deliveries later to a brilliant return *"caught and bowled"* catch from Sears.

The debutant's roar of delight was matched by the sell-out crowd who exploded with joy mere minutes later with the departure of Usman Khawaja brilliantly caught by a flying Tim Southee at 3rd Slip for just 11 and just 17 balls later, the debutant was at it again, forcing Cameron Green into an indecisive shot that saw him cannon the ball back onto his own middle stump.

Australia were 34-4 and rocking and rolling toward collapse.

Travis Head, so often Australia's saviour and attacking maestro with the bat nervously edged and prodded his way to 17 not out at the day ending *"Stumps"*, accompanied by a rather more assured run-a-ball 27 not out from the big hitting Mitchell Marsh and Australia ended day 3 in an unaccustomed underdog position for victory in this Test Match needing a further 202 runs to win tomorrow with only 6 wickets remaining. So the Kiwis hold sway in this second and final Test Match with their noisy neighbours and it's all to play for come Monday morning in Christchurch and Sunday night here in a rainy and cold England.

But rather more importantly for your favourite cricket correspondent, I have one final dance with this beautifully enticing and alluring sport that has had a hold of my heart for over four decades, and I can't wait to see how this final chapter of my winter odyssey will unfold later.

World Champion Aussies break Kiwi hearts again

New Zealand v Australia, 11th March 2024

NEW ZEALAND 162 all out and 372 all out

AUSTRALIA 256 all out and 281-7 (*Australia win by 3 wickets*)

What were you doing in 1993? Perhaps that isn't the question or indeed the opening gambit you were expecting for this, my final journal entry for an English Winter of watching cricket through the night, but Australia have broken their near neighbours cricketing hearts once more on their home turf and New Zealand's 31 year wait to triumph over their cousins from across the Tasman Sea continues. We'll get to Alex Carey's astonishing return to form with the bat and the Kiwis exciting approach to victory doused and extinguished by yet another stoic and determined performance from Aussie captain Pat Cummins soon enough, but as I started these journals this Winter with a New Zealand victory over England in India, the country of *"destiny"* in a World Cup they simply had to win on home soil but were thwarted by those pesky World Champion Australians, we seem to have come full circle, so why not luxuriate in a little time travelling back to the early 1990's too?

I may have started these journals in October of last year, filling them with tens of thousands of words and songs of praise for the grandest of all games, so perhaps it won't come as a shock to you that I've also watched far, far more cricket than I've actually appraised with my own written word. We'll return to 1993 shortly, but a Winter of watching Test Match cricket has also included the witnessing of Bangladesh shocking the world and New Zealand with their triumph by 150 runs as November tiptoed into the Christmas month of December, and a month full of cricket that saw Australia demolish a plucky if weak Pakistan 3–0 and either side of South Africa smashing India to pieces by an Innings and 32 runs. This match in beautiful Centurion ran concurrently with the always pleasing Boxing Day Test Match in the Coliseum of Melbourne's storied *"MCG"* and whilst India returned home to lick their wounds ahead of England's visit in the New Year, the West Indies arrived in Australia for a 2 match Test series that saw an expected crushing of the visitors by 10 wickets in the first match in Adelaide before Brisbane bore witness to one of the greatest matches in modern times and a cigarette paper thin West Indies victory by just 8 runs.

I watched it all, each and every match through the night, and back in a long ago 1993 I no doubt watched a large number of the 36 officially registered Test Matches that were played during a year also officially recognised as the *"International Year For The World's Indigenous People"*.

1993 saw out-going USA President George H W Bush sign an arms reduction treaty with Russian counterpart Boris Yeltsin before in-coming President Bill Clinton brokered the *"Oslo Accords"* between Israel and Palestine. The first attack on the World Trade Center resulted in the killing of 7 innocent human beings before ten times this number and many more were murdered in the siege of Waco, Texas. Czechoslovakia dissolved into the Czech Republic and Slovakia respectively, the moon was as near to earth as it would be until the year 2008 and *"Unforgiven"* won Best Picture at the 65th Academy Awards.

In April tennis superstar Monica Seles was horrifically stabbed at an event in Germany. June saw Kim Campbell sworn in as the first female Prime Minster of Canada. July saw a devastating tsunami in northern Japan tragically cost the lives of 230 people and in the final month of the year that saw the births (should you wish to feel old!) of Ariana Grande, Pete Davidson and Zayn Malik, drug cartel boss Pablo Escobar was shot and killed on a rooftop in Medellin, Colombia.

On the cricketing field of 1993, whilst England were losing a home Ashes series 4–1 to the auld enemy Australia as well as away series defeats in Sri Lanka (1–0) and India (3–0), the year started in spectacular fashion with a 1 run victory for the visiting West Indies in Adelaide, Australia, before coming to an end almost 11 months later with a 52 run victory for Pakistan on home territory in Rawalpindi against Zimbabwe and in between, my amateur cricketing exploits continued in the whites of *"Portsmouth Civil Service"* and a team I'd migrated into from my junior colt playing days.

I was always rather proud of being good enough as a young school-age teenager to play for the senior Men's team and now as a 21 year old fresh from college I spent every Sunday afternoon in the daunting company of men much older than myself. But I was an accomplished fast bowler in my youth and even if I say so myself, an integral member of a Sunday team that often crumbled to defeat yet I felt I belonged and appreciated on those long Summer afternoons of 1993 sunshine.

A season or more later I was swapping my childhood team for a cricketing gang of *"Zombies"* on a Sunday afternoon who despite their name were a ragtag bunch of ex semi-professionals and young would-be starlets whilst also playing cricket every Saturday afternoon too when not following Liverpool Football Club to yet another defeat and the proud captain of my work's team on cold, wet and windy Wednesday evenings following our sporting passions as we escaped the drudgery of a 9–5 existence inside a high-rise glassed box in the centre of the city.

Much has changed in the intervening 31 years: I left my hometown on the south coast of England for the central heartlands and wastelands of a long ago Industrial Revolution of the 18th Century. I became a father and travelled the furthest reaches of this Shakespearean Sceptred Isle in all directions of the compass in my search of vacuous corporate success as well as Premier League points for my beloved footballing love of Liverpool.

I've loved and I've lost.

I've watched from afar as the world has become ever more populated with vexatious players in a vaudevillian play in an upside down world that only eyes wide shut could possibly see.

I've lived in a historic *"toytown"* beside a gently rolling river and marvelled at the bells from the church atop a hill and barked at a full moon high above a *"Grand Old Lady"* and the world's oldest iron bridge.

I've said farewell to two of the kindest and loving ladies ever to grace this strange world of ours, in the words of Roy Batty *"I've seen things you people wouldn't believe"*, and I've watched a lot of Test Match cricket, a lot of Test Match cricket.

Which brings us in conclusion to last night or rather, a cold and wet morning of the future in New Zealand whereby Christchurch resembled Headingley in Yorkshire on a cold September day. The slate grey of Christchurch delayed the eagerly awaited 4th day's play by an hour and just under 4 hours later, and a final day in my cricket watching odyssey that had started out in rainfall, progressed to full, bright sunshine and now ended under rain filled clouds and beneath the glare of the *"Hagley Oval"* floodlights, Australia, against the odds, broke New Zealand hearts once more.

Starting the day in pursuit of 202 further runs for victory and with only 6 wickets in hand, Mitchell Marsh was granted a *"life"* from only the 7th delivery of the day as Rachin Ravindra dropped a simple if diving catch in the *"Gully"* position but after scampering a single, Travis Head perished from the very next ball in almost exactly the same manner but this time, Will Young safely pouched the catch. New Zealand, already heavy favourites entering day 4 were now firmly in control with Australia still needing 199 runs to win but to say Ravindra's dropped catch would be costly would be to heavily underestimate the 53 further runs Marsh would add in a 140 run partnership brilliantly dominated by Alex Carey.

The wicket-keeper batsman would himself be granted a *"life"* when given out LBW on 19 but Matt Henry's brilliant in-swinging delivery had, in the cricketing vernacular for the final time in these journals, *"done too much"* and after his reprieve from the TV umpire, Carey simply didn't look back. The 32 year old from Loxton is forever under pressure for his place in this Australian team and was rather shell-shocked by the outlandish criticism bowled his way following last Summer's infamous dismissal of Jonny Bairstow in the Ashes. I championed him then for his quick thinking and I'll forever praise him now for a battling innings of 50 from 61 balls received and although he'd eventually finish 2 runs shy of a Test Match century, he couldn't wait to celebrate with his captain as he hit the winning runs to cap a remarkable 3 wicket victory.

New Zealand debutant Ben Sears threatened to turn the already written script above upside down by dismissing Mitchell Marsh and Mitchell Starc in consecutive balls to set up both a hat-trick opportunity and leave Australia still needing 59 runs for victory. But step forward, once again, Aussie captain Pat Cummins with a serene 32 runs from 44 balls and with Carey gliding along at the other end, Australia, as they always seem to do, ripped a victory from the jaws of almost certain defeat.

I wanted the Kiwis to win but I didn't have a real dog in the fight. I was just grateful for yet another opportunity to watch Test Match cricket through the night and a final chapter of my Winter odyssey had a rather fitting, sporting conclusion.

Sundries on the Scorecard

It's been 9 days since I last watched any Test Match cricket so you'll forgive me if I ramble and muse disorderly through some final musings here. The chocolate biscuit intake remains on as steady a trajectory as my ability to make and drink tea but the added ingredient of Test Match cricket is missing, and I guess I need my fix. I pen these words not 24 hours since my glorious football team were involved in one of the greatest games of football seen on free to air television for many a long football season. They emerged defeated from a headline writer's *"7 goal thriller"* having actually *"won"* the game, twice, before conspiring to lose it, twice, and finally, in the final minute of extra-time. In another lifetime my dear old Mum, one of THE main reasons why I obsess over the grand old game of cricket, would have watched and cheered this ridiculous game of football, and for a victory for the team she adored. I always think of that grand old lady when watching cricket and for the love of this great game she nurtured before allowing it to flower in my own obsessive way. She also had the great foresight to bathe me in the correct footballing faith and those mighty footballing goliaths dressed all in Red who thrilled a TV nation, snatching defeat from the jaws of certain victory.

I hope you were watching Mum.

I've watched way above an average amount of films since beginning this odyssey on 5th October, been accompanied on many a stroll along the banks of the River Severn by my son and towards the end of 5 months of indulgence, I've reacquainted myself with many picturesque sections of the canal that winds its way through the County. I've tried to record an audio book.

The key word in that sentence being *"tried"*.

Christmas came and went and along with it yet another Boxing Day Test Match from the field of dreams that is the Melbourne Cricket Ground, and I became another year older in this game we call life as I dreamed dreams of sitting in beautiful Mount Maunganui, and thanking my lucky stars. I'm self-publishing my sixth book in the Summer and by which time I will have returned to my spiritual home of Ironbridge a number of times, hopefully watched my Mum's second favourite football team give their genial German manager a silver trophy lining for his heart breaking departure, and I'll have continued watching far too many films.

The revolutionaries are home and/or flying to all parts of the cricketing world for the colourful short form of the game now played the world over. Cricket is now a year round sport with a prime calendar slot reserved for the longer form, pun intended test, of the grand old game.

West Indies and Sri Lanka visit in the Summer before the revolutionaries set sail for New Zealand in December and another excuse for me to drink tea and eat far too many chocolate biscuits in the middle of the night.

News post-tour is rather thin on the ground.

A straw poll from a smattering of headlines I've seen and quickly ignored centre as you'd imagine on *"Bazball"*, senior cricket figures of the past (who shall remain nameless) severely critical of Ben Stokes and his captaincy of the England team (nothing new) and at the time of writing, James *"Jimmy"* Anderson still hasn't called father time on his Test Match cricket career, and long may that continue.

In the absence therefore of any written substance with which to conclude this elongated thank you for buying this book, we'll turn in conclusion to England coach Brendon McCullum for some final rambling musings.

Amid the highest of praise for a wonderful India team, McCullum was starkly honest in an interview for the BBC radio institution that is *"Test Match Special"* as he admitted to his team being ***"exposed"*** and ***"timid"*** towards the end of this eight week period and yet ***"a lot of good will come out of this tour"***.

McCullum and captain Stokes have turned around a perennially losing team into a successful winning one aside from the two toughest assignments in world cricket. McCullum desires a ***"more refined version"*** of his team of revolutionaries and a team that ***"has to move forward"*** in an evolution abundant with talented, eager replacements for every position in the team. The genial Kiwi talked of ***"not backing down"*** and from ***"rocks"*** and ***"diamonds"*** he and Stokes will continue to craft their revolutionary team. I always enjoy listening to Brendon McCullum and whilst these are my words now and not his, he bubbled over as always with enthusiasm for the very game of Test Match cricket and he wants to play an exciting, thrilling brand of cricket that will pay due homage to the game whilst rocketing it into the public consciousness. McCullum, like Indian counterpart Rahul Dravid, his captain Rohit Sharma and his on field skipper Ben Stokes, they all have a reverence for the grand old game I can only applaud. Test Match cricket has a colourful year round competitor now, but these four men speak so well as to why Test Match cricket is so very special.

Vive la révolution!

I can't thank you sincerely enough for reading and I hope you've enjoyed the ride.

Stephen Blackford
18th March 2024

Printed in Great Britain
by Amazon